The Philanderer

By

George Bernard Shaw

The Echo Library 2006

Published by

The Echo Library

Echo Library
131 High St.
Teddington
Middlesex TW11 8HH

www.echo-library.com

Please report serious faults in the text to complaints@echo-library.com

ISBN 1-40680-532-7

ACT I

A lady and gentleman are making love to one another in the drawing-room of a flat in Ashly Gardens in the Victoria district of London. It is past ten at night. The walls are hung with theatrical engravings and photographs—Kemble as Hamlet, Mrs. Siddons as Queen Katharine pleading in court, Macready as Werner *(after Maclise)*, Sir Henry Irving as Richard III *(after Long)*, Miss Ellen Terry, Mrs. Kendal, Miss Ada Rehan, Madame Sarah Bernhardt, Mr. Henry Arthur Jones, Mr. A. W. Pinero, Mr. Sydney Grundy, and so on, but not the Signora Duse or anyone connected with Ibsen. The room is not a perfect square, the right hand corner at the back being cut off diagonally by the doorway, and the opposite corner rounded by a turret window filled up with a stand of flowers surrounding a statue of Shakespear. The fireplace is on the right, with an armchair near it. A small round table, further forward on the same side, with a chair beside it, has a yellow-backed French novel lying open on it. The piano, a grand, is on the left, open, with the keyboard in full view at right angles to the wall. The piece of music on the desk is "When other lips." Incandescent lights, well shaded, are on the piano and mantelpiece. Near the piano is a sofa, on which the lady and gentleman are seated affectionately side by side, in one another's arms.

The lady, Grace Tranfield, is about 32, slight of build, delicate of feature, and sensitive in expression. She is just now given up to the emotion of the moment; but her well closed mouth, proudly set brows, firm chin, and elegant carriage show plenty of determination and self respect. She is in evening dress.

The gentleman, Leonard Charteris, a few years older, is unconventionally but smartly dressed in a velvet jacket and cashmere trousers. His collar, dyed Wotan blue, is part of his shirt, and turns over a garnet coloured scarf of Indian silk, secured by a turquoise ring. He wears blue socks and leather sandals. The arrangement of his tawny hair, and of his moustaches and short beard, is apparently left to Nature; but he has taken care that Nature shall do him the fullest justice. His amative enthusiasm, at which he is himself laughing, and his clever, imaginative, humorous ways, contrast strongly with the sincere tenderness and dignified quietness of the woman.

CHARTERIS *(impulsively clasping Grace)*. My dearest love.
GRACE *(responding affectionately)*. My darling. Are you happy?
CHARTERIS. In Heaven.
GRACE. My own.
CHARTERIS. My heart's love. *(He sighs happily, and takes her hands in his, looking quaintly at her.)* That must positively be my last kiss, Grace, or I shall become downright silly. Let us talk. *(Releases her and sits a little apart from her.)* Grace: is this your first love affair?
GRACE. Have you forgotten that I am a widow? Do you think I married Tranfield for money?
CHARTERIS. How do I know? Besides, you might have married him not

because you loved him, but because you didn't love anybody else. When one is young, one marries out of mere curiosity, just to see what it's like.

GRACE. Well, since you ask me, I never was in love with Tranfield, though I only found that out when I fell in love with you. But I used to like him for being in love with me. It brought out all the good in him so much that I have wanted to be in love with some one ever since. I hope, now that I am in love with you, you will like me for it just as I liked Tranfield.

CHARTERIS. My dear, it is because I like you that I want to marry you. I could love anybody—any pretty woman, that is.

GRACE. Do you really mean that, Leonard?

CHARTERIS. Of course. Why not?

GRACE (reflecting). Never mind why. Now tell me, is this your first love affair?

CHARTERIS (amazed at the simplicity of the question). No, bless my soul. No— nor my second, nor my third.

GRACE. But I mean your first serious one.

CHARTERIS (with a certain hesitation). Yes. (There is a pause. She is not convinced. He adds, with a very perceptible load on his conscience.) It is the first in which I have been serious.

GRACE (searchingly). I see. The other parties were always serious.

CHARTERIS. No, not always—heaven forbid!

GRACE. How often?

CHARTERIS. Well, once.

GRACE. Julia Craven?

CHARTERIS (recoiling). Who told you that? (She shakes her head mysteriously, and he turns away from her moodily and adds) You had much better not have asked.

GRACE (gently). I'm sorry, dear. (She puts out her hand and pulls softly at him to bring him near her again.)

CHARTERIS (yielding mechanically to the pull, and allowing her hand to rest on his arm, but sitting squarely without the least attempt to return the caress). Do I feel harder to the touch than I did five minutes ago?

GRACE. What nonsense!

CHARTERIS. I feel as if my body had turned into the toughest of hickory. That is what comes of reminding me of Julia Craven. (Brooding, with his chin on his right hand and his elbow on his knee.) I have sat alone with her just as I am sitting with you—

GRACE (shrinking from him). Just!

CHARTERIS (sitting upright and facing her steadily). Just exactly. She has put her hands in mine, and laid her cheek against mine, and listened to me saying all sorts of silly things. (Grace, chilled to the soul, rises from the sofa and sits down on the piano stool, with her back to the keyboard.) Ah, you don't want to hear any more of the story. So much the better.

GRACE (deeply hurt, but controlling herself). When did you break it off?

CHARTERIS (guiltily). Break it off?

GRACE (firmly). Yes, break it off.

CHARTERIS. Well, let me see. When did I fall in love with you?

GRACE. Did you break it off then?

CHARTERIS (*mischievously, making it plainer and plainer that it has not been broken off*). It was clear then, of course, that it must be broken off.

GRACE. And did you break it off?

CHARTERIS. Oh, yes: I broke it off,

GRACE. But did she break it off?

CHARTERIS (*rising*). As a favour to me, dearest, change the subject. Come away from the piano: I want you to sit here with me. (*Takes a step towards her.*)

GRACE. No. I also have grown hard to the touch—much harder than hickory for the present. Did she break it off?

CHARTERIS. My dear, be reasonable. It was fully explained to her that it was to be broken off.

GRACE. Did she accept the explanation?

CHARTERIS. She did what a woman like Julia always does. When I explained personally, she said it was not not my better self that was speaking, and that she knew I still really loved her. When I wrote it to her with brutal explicitness, she read the letter carefully and then sent it back to me with a note to say that she had not had the courage to open it, and that I ought to be ashamed of having written it. (*Comes beside Grace, and puts his left hand caressingly round her neck.*) You see, dearie, she won't look the situation in the face.

GRACE. (*shaking off his hand and turning a little away on the stool*). I am afraid, from the light way in which you speak of it, you did not sound the right chord.

CHARTERIS. My dear, when you are doing what a woman calls breaking her heart, you may sound the very prettiest chords you can find on the piano; but to her ears it is just like this—(*Sits down on the bass end of the keyboard. Grace puts her fingers in her ears. He rises and moves away from the piano, saying*) No, my dear: I've been kind; I've been frank; I've been everything that a goodnatured man could be: she only takes it as the making up of a lover's quarrel. (*Grace winces.*) Frankness and kindness: one is as the other—especially frankness. I've tried both. (*He crosses to the fireplace, and stands facing the fire, looking at the ornaments on the mantelpiece and warming his hands.*)

GRACE (*Her voice a little strained*). What are you going to try now?

CHARTERIS (*on the hearthrug, turning to face her*). Action, my dear! Marriage!! In that she must believe. She won't be convinced by anything short of it, because, you see, I have had some tremendous philanderings before and have gone back to her after them.

GRACE. And so that is why you want to marry me?

CHARTERIS. I cannot deny it, my love. Yes: it is your mission to rescue me from Julia.

GRACE (*rising*). Then, if you please, I decline to be made use of for any such purpose. I will not steal you from another woman. (*She begins to walk up and down the room with ominous disquiet.*)

CHARTERIS. Steal me! (*Comes towards her.*) Grace: I have a question to put to you as an advanced woman. Mind! as an advanced woman. Does Julia belong to me? Am I her owner—her master?

GRACE. Certainly not. No woman is the property of a man. A woman belongs to herself and to nobody else.

CHARTERIS. Quite right. Ibsen for ever! That's exactly my opinion. Now tell me, do I belong to Julia; or have I a right to belong to myself?

GRACE *(puzzled)*. Of course you have; but—

CHARTERIS *(interrupting her triumphantly)*. Then how can you steal me from Julia if I don't belong to her? *(Catching her by the shoulders and holding her out at arm's length in front of him.)* Eh, little philosopher? No, my dear: if Ibsen sauce is good for the goose, it's good for the gander as well. Besides *(coaxing her)* it was nothing but a philander with Julia—nothing else in the world, I assure you.

GRACE *(breaking away from him)*. So much the worse! I hate your philanderings: they make me ashamed of you and of myself. *(Goes to the sofa and sits in the right hand corner of it, leaning gloomily on her elbow with her face averted.)*

CHARTERIS. Grace: you utterly misunderstand the origin of my philanderings. *(Sits down beside her.)* Listen to me: am I a particularly handsome man?

GRACE *(turning to him as if astonished at his conceit)*. No!

CHARTERIS *(triumphantly)*. You admit it. Am I a well dressed man?

GRACE. Not particularly.

CHARTERIS. Of course not. Have I a romantic mysterious charm about me?—do I look as if a secret sorrow preyed on me?—am I gallant to women?

GRACE. Not in the least.

CHARTERIS. Certainly not. No one can accuse me of it. Then whose fault is it that half the women I speak to fall in love with me? Not mine: I hate it: it bores me to distraction. At first it flattered me—delighted me—that was how Julia got me, because she was the first woman who had the pluck to make me a declaration. But I soon had enough of it; and at no time have I taken the initiative and persecuted women with my advances as women have persecuted me. Never. Except, of course, in your case.

GRACE. Oh, you need not make any exception. I had a good deal of trouble to induce you to come and see us. You were very coy.

CHARTERIS *(fondly, taking her hand)*. With you, dearest, the coyness was sheer coquetry. I loved you from the first, and fled only that you might pursue. But come! let us talk about something really interesting. *(Takes her in his arms.)* Do you love me better than anyone else in the world?

GRACE. I don't think you like to be loved too much.

CHARTERIS. That depends on who the person is. You *(pressing her to his heart)* cannot love me too much: you cannot love me half enough. I reproach you every day for your coldness—your— *(Violent double knock heard without. They start and listen, still in one another's arms, hardly daring to breathe.)* Who the deuce is calling at this hour?

GRACE. I can't imagine. *(They listen guiltily. The door of the flat is opened without. They hastily get away from one another.)*

A WOMAN'S VOICE OUTSIDE. Is Mr. Charteris here?

CHARTERIS *(springing up)*. Julia! The devil! *(Stands at the left of the sofa with his hands on it, bending forward with his eyes fixed on the door.)*

GRACE *(rising also)*. What can she want?

THE VOICE. Never mind: I will announce myself. *(A beautiful, dark, tragic looking woman, in mantle and bonnet, appears at the door, raging furiously.)* Oh, this is charming. I have interrupted a pretty tete-a-tete. Oh, you villain! *(She comes straight at Grace. Charteris runs across behind the sofa and stops her. She struggles furiously with him. Grace preserves her self possession, but retreats quietly to the piano. Julia, finding Charteris too strong for her, gives up her attempt to get at Grace, but strikes him in the face as she frees herself.)*

CHARTERIS *(shocked)*. Oh, Julia, Julia! This is too bad.

JULIA. Is it, indeed, too bad? What are you doing up here with that woman? You scoundrel! But now listen to me; Leonard: you have driven me to desperation; and I don't care what I do, or who hears me. I'll not bear it. She shall not have my place with you—

CHARTERIS. Sh-sh!

JULIA. No, no: I don't care: I will expose her true character before everybody. You belong to me: you have no right to be here; and she knows it.

CHARTERIS. I think you had better let me take you home, Julia.

JULIA. I will not. I am not going home: I am going to stay here—here— until I have made you give her up.

CHARTERIS. My dear, you must be reasonable. You really cannot stay in Mrs. Tranfield's house if she objects. She can ring the bell and have us both put out.

JULIA. Let her do it then. Let her ring the bell if she dares. Let us see how this pure virtuous creature will face the scandal of what I will declare about her. Let us see how you will face it. I have nothing to lose. Everybody knows how you have treated me: you have boasted of your conquests, you poor pitiful, vain creature—I am the common talk of your acquaintances and hers. Oh, I have calculated my advantage *(tearing off her mantle)*: I am a most unhappy and injured woman; but I am not the fool you take me to be. I am going to stay—see! *(She flings the mantle on the round table; puts her bonnet on it, and sits down.)* Now, Mrs. Tranfield: there is the bell: *(pointing to the button beside the fireplace)* why don't you ring? *(Grace, looking attentively at Charteris, does not move.)* Ha! ha! I thought so.

CHARTERIS *(quietly, without relaxing his watch on Julia)*. Mrs. Tranfield: I think you had better go into another room. *(Grace makes a movement towards the door, but stops and looks inquiringly at Charteris as Julia springs up. He advances a step so as to prevent her from getting to the door.)*

JULIA. She shall not. She shall stay here. She shall know what you are, and how you have been in love with me—how it is not two days since you kissed me and told me that the future would be as happy as the past. *(Screaming at him)* You did: deny it if you dare.

CHARTERIS *(to Grace in a low voice)*. Go!

GRACE *(with nonchalant disgust—going)*. Get her away as soon as you can, Leonard.

(Julia, with a stifled cry of rage, rushes at Grace, who is crossing behind the sofa towards

door. Charteris seizes her and prevents her from getting past the sofa. Grace goes out. Charteris, holding Julia fast, looks around to the door to see whether Grace is safely out of the room.)

JULIA *(suddenly ceasing to struggle and speaking with the most pathetic dignity)*. Oh, there is no need to be violent. *(He passes her across to the left end of the sofa, and leans against the right end, panting and mopping his forehead)*. That is worthy of you!—to use brute force—to humiliate me before her! *(She breaks down and bursts into tears.)*

CHARTERIS *(to himself with melancholy conviction)*. This is going to be a cheerful evening. Now patience, patience, patience! *(Sits on a chair near the round table.)*

JULIA *(in anguish)*. Leonard, have you no feeling for me?

CHARTERIS. Only an intense desire to get you safely out of this.

JULIA *(fiercely)*. I am not going to stir.

CHARTERIS *(wearily)*. Well, well. *(Heaves a long sigh. They sit silent for awhile, Julia struggling, not to regain her self control, but to maintain her rage at boiling point.)*

JULIA *(rising suddenly)*. I am going to speak to that woman.

CHARTERIS *(jumping up)*. No, no. Hang it, Julia, don't let's have another wrestling match. I have the strength, but not the wind: you're too young for me. Sit down or else let me take you home. Suppose her father comes in.

JULIA. I don't care. It rests with you. I am ready to go if she will give you up: until then I stay. Those are my terms: you owe me that, *(She sits down determinedly. Charteris looks at her for a moment; then, making up his mind, goes resolutely to the couch, sits down near the right hand end of it, she being at the left; and says with biting emphasis)*—

CHARTERIS. I owe you just exactly nothing.

JULIA *(reproachfully)*. Nothing! You can look me in the face and say that? Oh, Leonard!

CHARTERIS. Let me remind you, Julia, that when first we became acquainted, the position you took up was that of a woman of advanced views.

JULIA. That should have made you respect me the more.

CHARTERIS *(placably)*. So it did, my dear. But that is not the point. As a woman of advanced views, you were determined to be free. You regarded marriage as a degrading bargain, by which a woman sold herself to a man for the social status of a wife and the right to be supported and pensioned in old age out of his income. That's the advanced view—our view. Besides, if you had married me, I might have turned out a drunkard, a criminal, an imbecile, a horror to you; and you couldn't have released yourself. Too big a risk, you see. That's the rational view—our view. Accordingly, you reserved the right to leave me at any time if you found our companionship incompatible with—what was the expression you used?—with your full development as a human being: I think that was how you put the Ibsenist view—our view. So I had to be content with a charming philander, which taught me a great deal, and brought me some hours of exquisite happiness.

JULIA. Leonard: you confess then that you owe me something?

CHARTERIS *(haughtily)*. No: what I received, I paid. Did you learn nothing from me?—was there no delight for you in our friendship?

JULIA (*vehemently and movingly; for she is now sincere*). No. You made me pay dearly for every moment of happiness. You revenged yourself on me for the humiliation of being the slave of your passion for me. I was never sure of you for a moment. I trembled whenever a letter came from you, lest it should contain some stab for me. I dreaded your visits almost as much as I longed for them. I was your plaything, not your companion. (*She rises, exclaiming*) Oh, there was such suffering in my happiness that I hardly knew joy from pain. (*She sinks on the piano stool, and adds, as she buries her face in her hands and turns away from him*) Better for me if I had never met you!

CHARTERIS (*rising indignantly*). You ungenerous wretch! Is this your gratitude for the way I have just been flattering you? What have I not endured from you—endured with angelic patience? Did I not find out, before our friendship was a fortnight old, that all your advanced views were merely a fashion picked up and followed like any other fashion, without understanding or meaning a word of them? Did you not, in spite of your care for your own liberty, set up claims on me compared to which the claims of the most jealous wife would have been trifles. Have I a single woman friend whom you have not abused as old, ugly, vicious—

JULIA (*quickly looking up*). So they are.

CHARTERIS. Well, then, I'll come to grievances that even you can understand. I accuse you of habitual and intolerable jealousy and ill temper; of insulting me on imaginary provocation: of positively beating me; of stealing letters of mine—

JULIA (*rising*). Yes, nice letters.

CHARTERIS. —of breaking your solemn promises not to do it again; of spending hours—aye, days! piecing together the contents of my waste paper basket in your search for more letters; and then representing yourself as an ill used saint and martyr wantonly betrayed and deserted by a selfish monster of a man.

JULIA. I was justified in reading your letters. Our perfect confidence in one another gave me the right to do it.

CHARTERIS. Thank you. Then I hasten to break off a confidence which gives such rights. (*Sits down sulkily on sofa.*)

JULIA (*with her right hand on the back of the sofa, bending over him threateningly*). You have no right to break it off.

CHARTERIS. I have. You refused to marry me because—

JULIA. I did not. You never asked me. If we were married, you would never dare treat me as you are doing now.

CHARTERIS (*laboriously going back to his argument*). It was understood between us as people of advanced views that we were not to marry because, as the law stands, I might have become a drunkard, a—

JULIA. —a criminal, an imbecile or a horror. You said that before. (*Sits down beside him with a fling.*)

CHARTERIS (*politely*). I beg your pardon, my dear. I know I have a habit of repeating myself. The point is that you reserved your freedom to give me up when you pleased.

JULIA. Well, what of that? I do not please to give you up; and I will not. You have not become a drunkard or a criminal.

CHARTERIS. You don't see the point yet, Julia. You seem to forget that in reserving your freedom to leave me in case I should turn out badly, you also reserved my freedom to leave you in case you should turn out badly.

JULIA. Very ingenious. And pray, have *I* become a drunkard, or a criminal, or an imbecile?

CHARTERIS (*rising*). You have become what is infinitely worse than all three together—a jealous termagant.

JULIA (*shaking her head bitterly*). Yes, abuse me—call me names.

CHARTERIS. I now assert the right I reserved—the right of breaking with you when I please. Advanced views, Julia, involve advanced duties: you cannot be an advanced woman when you want to bring a man to your feet, and a conventional woman when you want to hold him there against his will. Advanced people form charming friendships: conventional people marry. Marriage suits a good deal of people; and its first duty is fidelity. Friendship suits some people; and its first duty is unhesitating, uncomplaining acceptance of a notice of a change of feeling from either side. You chose friendship instead of marriage. Now do your duty, and accept your notice.

JULIA. Never! We are engaged in the eye of—the eye of—

CHARTERIS (*sitting down quickly beside her*). Yes, Julia. Can't you get it out? In the eye of something that advanced women don't believe in, en?

JULIA (*throwing herself at his feet*). O Leonard, don't be cruel. I am too miserable to argue—to think. I only know I love you. You reproach me with not wanting to marry you. I would have married you at any time after I came to love you, if you had asked me. I will marry you now if you will.

CHARTERIS. I won't, my dear. That's flat. We're intellectually incompatible.

JULIA. But why? We could be so happy. You love me—I know you love me—I feel it. You say "My dear" to me: you have said it several times this evening. I know I have been wicked, odious, bad. I say nothing in defence of myself. But don't be hard on me. I was distracted by the thought of losing you. I can't face life without you Leonard. I was happy when I met you: I had never loved anyone; and if you had only let me alone I could have gone on contentedly by myself. But I can't now. I must have you with me. Don't cast me off without a thought of all I have at stake. I could be a friend to you if you would only let me—if you would only tell me your plans—give me a share in your work—treat me as something more than the amusement of an idle hour. Oh Leonard, Leonard, you've never given me a chance: indeed you haven't. I'll take pains; I'll read; I'll try to think; I'll conquer my jealousy; I'll— (*She breaks down, rocking her head desperately on his knee and writhing.*) Oh, I'm mad: I'm mad: you'll kill me if you desert me.

CHARTERIS (*petting her*). My dear love, don't cry—don't go on in this way. You know I can't help it.

JULIA (*sobbing as he rises and coaxingly lifts her with him*). Oh, you can, you can. One word from you will make us happy for ever.

CHARTERIS (*diplomatically*). Come, my dear: we really must go. We can't stay until Cuthbertson comes. (*Releases her gently and takes her mantle from the table.*) Here is your mantle: put it on and be good. You have given me a terrible evening: you must have some consideration for me.

JULIA (*dangerous again*). Then I am to be cast off.

CHARTERIS (*coaxingly*). You are to put on your bonnet, dearest. (*He puts the mantle on her shoulders.*)

JULIA (*with a bitter half laugh, half sob*). Well, I suppose I must do what I am told. (*She goes to the table, and looks for her bonnet. She sees the yellow-backed French novel.*) Ah, look at that! (*holds it out to him.*) Look—look at what the creature reads—filthy, vile French stuff that no decent woman would touch. And you—you have been reading it with her.

CHARTERIS. You recommended that book to me yourself.

JULIA. Faugh! (*Dashes it on the floor.*)

CHARTERIS (*running anxiously to the book*). Don't damage property, Julia. (*He picks it up and dusts it.*) Making scenes is an affair of sentiment: damaging property is serious. (*Replaces it on the table.*) And now do pray come along.

JULIA (*implacably*). You can go: there is nothing to prevent you. I will not stir. (*She sits down stubbornly on the sofa.*)

CHARTERIS (*losing patience*). Oh come! I am not going to begin all this over again. There are limits even to my forbearance. Come on.

JULIA. I will not, I tell you.

CHARTERIS. Then good night. (*He makes resolutely for the door. With a rush, she gets there before him, and bars his way.*) I thought you wanted me to go.

JULIA (*at the door*). You shall not leave me here alone.

CHARTERIS. Then come with me.

JULIA. Not until you have sworn to me to give up that woman.

CHARTERIS. My dear, I will swear anything if you will only come away and put an end to this.

JULIA (*perplexed—doubting him*). You will swear?

CHARTERIS. Solemnly. Propose the oath. I have been on the point of swearing for the last half hour.

JULIA (*despairingly*). You are only making fun of me. I want no oaths. I want your promise—your sacred word of honour.

CHARTERIS. Certainly anything you demand, on condition that you come away immediately. On my sacred word of honour as a gentleman—as an Englishman—as anything you like—I will never see her again, never speak to her, never think of her. Now come.

JULIA. But are you in earnest? Will you keep your word?

CHARTERIS (*smiling subtly*). Now you are getting unreasonable. Do come along without any more nonsense. At any rate, I am going. I am not strong enough to carry you home; but I am strong enough to make my way through that door in spite of you. You will then have a new grievance against me for my brutal violence. *(He takes a step towards the door.)*

JULIA *(solemnly)*. If you do, I swear I will throw myself from that window, Leonard, as you pass out.

CHARTERIS *(unimpressed)*. That window is at the back of the building. I shall pass out at the front; so you will not hurt me. Good night. *(He approaches the door.)*

JULIA. Leonard: have you no pity?

CHARTERIS. Not in the least. When you condescend to these antics you force me to despise you. How can a woman who behaves like a spoiled child and talks like a sentimental novel have the audacity to dream of being a companion for a man of any sort of sense or character? *(She gives an inarticulate cry and throws herself sobbing on his breast.)* Come, don't cry, my dear Julia: you don't look half so beautiful as when you're happy; and it takes all the starch out of my shirt front. Come along.

JULIA *(affectionately)*. I'll come, dear, if you wish it. Give me one kiss.

CHARTERIS *(exasperated)*. This is too much. No: I'm dashed if I will. Here, let me go, Julia. *(She clings to him.)* Will you come without another word if I give you a kiss?

JULIA. I will do anything you wish, darling.

CHARTERIS. Well, here. *(He takes her in his arms and gives her an unceremonious kiss.)* Now remember your promise. Come along.

JULIA. That was not a nice kiss, dearest. I want one of our old real kisses.

CHARTERIS *(furious)*. Oh, go to the deuce. *(He disengages himself impulsively; and she, as if he had flung her down, falls pathetically with a stifled moan. With an angry look at her, he strides out and slams the door. She raises herself on one hand, listening to his retreating footsteps. They stop. Her face lights up with eager, triumphant cunning. The steps return hastily. She throws herself down again as before. Charteris reappears, in the utmost dismay, exclaiming)* Julia: we're done. Cuthbertson's coming upstairs with your father—*(she sits up quickly)* do you hear?—the two fathers.

JULIA *(sitting on the floor)*. Impossible. They don't know one another.

CHARTERIS *(desperately)*. I tell you they are coming up together like brothers. What on earth are we to do?

JULIA *(scrambling up with the help of his hand)*. Quick, the lift: we can go down in that. *(She rushes to the table for her bonnet.)*

CHARTERIS. No, the man's gone home; and the lift's locked.

JULIA *(putting on bonnet at express speed)*. Let's go up to the next floor.

CHARTERIS. There's no next floor. We're at the top of the house. No, no, you must invent some thumping lie. I can't think of one: you can, Julia. Exercise all your genius. I'll back you up.

JULIA. But——

CHARTERIS. Sh-sh! Here they are. Sit down and look at home. *(Julia tears off her bonnet and mantle; throws them on the table; and darts to the piano at which she seats herself.)*

JULIA. Come and sing. *(She plays the symphony to "When other lips." He stands at the piano, as if about to sing. Two elderly gentlemen enter. Julia stops playing.)*

The elder of the two gentlemen, Colonel Daniel Craven, affects the bluff, simple veteran, and carries it off pleasantly and well, having a fine upright figure, and being, in fact, a goodnaturedly impulsive, credulous person who, after an entirely thoughtless career as an officer and a gentleman, is now being startled into some sort of self-education by the surprising proceedings of his children.

His companion, Mr. Joseph Cuthbertson, Grace's father, has none of the Colonel's boyishness. He is a man of fervent idealistic sentiment, so frequently outraged by the facts of life, that he has acquired an habitually indignant manner, which unexpectedly becomes enthusiastic or affectionate when he speaks.

The two men differ greatly in expression. The Colonel's face is lined with weather, with age, with eating and drinking, and with the cumulative effects of many petty vexations, but not with thought: he is still fresh, and he has by no means full expectations of pleasure and novelty. Cuthbertson has the lines of sedentary London brain work, with its chronic fatigue and longing for rest and recreative emotion, and its disillusioned indifference to adventure and enjoyment, except as a means of recuperation.

They are both in evening dress; and Cuthbertson wears his fur collared overcoat, which, with his vigilant, irascible eye, piled up hair, and the honorable earnestness with which he takes himself, gives him an air of considerable consequence.

CUTHBERTSON (with a hospitable show of delight at finding visitors). Don't stop, Miss Craven. Go on, Charteris. (He comes down behind the sofa, and hangs his overcoat on it, after taking an opera glass and a theatre programme from the pockets, and putting them down on the piano. Craven meanwhile goes to the fire-place and stands on the hearthrug.)

CHARTERIS. No, thank you. Miss Craven has just been taking me through an old song; and I've had enough of it. (He takes the song off the piano desk and lays it aside; then closes the lid over the keyboard.)

JULIA (passing between the sofa and piano to shake hands with Cuthbertson). Why, you've brought Daddy! What a surprise! (Looking across to Craven.) So glad you've come, Dad. (She takes a chair near the window, and sits there.)

CUTHBERTSON. Craven: let me introduce you to Mr. Leonard Charteris, the famous Ibsenist philosopher.

CRAVEN. Oh, we know one another already. Charteris is quite at home at our house, Jo.

CUTHBERTSON. I beg both your pardons. (Charteris sits down on the piano stool.) He's quite at home here too. By the bye, where's Grace?

JULIA and CHARTERIS. Er— (They stop and look at one another.)

JULIA (politely). I beg your pardon, Mr. Charteris: I interrupted you.

CHARTERIS. Not at all, Miss Craven. (An awkward pause.)

CUTHBERTSON (to help them out). You were going to tell about Grace, Charteris.

CHARTERIS. I was only going to say that I didn't know that you and Craven were acquainted.

CRAVEN. Why, *I* didn't know it until to-night. It's a most extraordinary thing. We met by chance at the theatre; and he turns out to be my oldest friend.

CUTHBERTSON *(energetically)*. Yes, Craven; and do you see how this proves what I was saying to you about the breaking up of family life? Here are all our young people—Grace and Miss Julia and the rest—bosom friends, inseparables; and yet we two, who knew each other before they were born, might never have met again if you hadn't popped into the stall next to mine to-night by pure chance. Come, sit down *(bustling over to him affectionately and pushing him into the arm chair above the fire)*: there's your place, by my fireside, whenever you choose to fill it. *(He posts himself at the right end of the sofa, leaning against it and admiring Craven.)* Just imagine your being Dan Craven!

CRAVEN. Just imagine your being Jo Cuthbertson, though! That's a far more extraordinary coincidence, because I'd got it into my head that your name was Tranfield.

CUTHBERTSON. Oh, that's my daughter's name. She's a widow, you know. How uncommonly well you look, Dan! The years haven't hurt you much.

CRAVEN *(suddenly becoming unnaturally gloomy)*. I look well. I even feel well. But my days are numbered.

CUTHBERTSON *(alarmed)*. Oh don't say that, my dear fellow. I hope not.

JULIA *(with anguish in her voice)*. Daddy! *(Cuthbertson looks inquiringly around at her.)*

CRAVEN. There, there, my dear: I was wrong to talk of it. It's a sad subject. But it's better that Cuthbertson should know. We used to be very close friends, and are so still, I hope. *(Cuthbertson goes to Craven and presses his hand silently; then returns to sofa and sits, pulling out his handkerchief and displaying some emotion.)*

CHARTERIS *(a little impatiently)*. The fact is, Cuthbertson, Craven's a devout believer in the department of witchcraft called medical science. He's celebrated in all the medical schools as an example of the newest sort of liver complaint. The doctors say he can't last another year; and he has fully made up his mind not to survive next Easter, just to oblige them.

CRAVEN *(with military affectation)*. It's very kind of you to try to keep up my spirits by making light of it, Charteris. But I shall be ready when my time comes. I'm a soldier. *(A sob from Julia.)* Don't cry, Julia.

CUTHBERTSON *(huskily)*. I hope you may long be spared, Dan.

CRAVEN. To oblige me, Jo, change the subject. *(He gets up and again posts himself on the hearthrug with his back to the fire.)*

CHARTERIS. Try and persuade him to join our club, Cuthbertson. He mopes.

JULIA. It's no use. Sylvia and I are always at him to join; but he won't.

CRAVEN. My child, I have my own club.

CHARTERIS *(contemptuously)*. Yes, the Junior Army and Navy! Do you call that a club? Why, they daren't let a woman cross the doorstep!

CRAVEN *(a little ruffled)*. Clubs are a matter of taste, Charteris. You like a cock and hen club: I don't. It's bad enough to have Julia and her sister—a girl under twenty—spending half their time at such a place. Besides, now really, such a name for a club! The Ibsen club! I should be laughed out of London. The Ibsen club! Come, Cuthbertson, back me up. I'm sure you agree with me.

CHARTERIS. Cuthbertson's a member.

CRAVEN (*amazed*). No! Why, he's been talking to me all the evening about the way in which everything is going to the dogs through advanced ideas in the younger generation.

CHARTERIS. Of course. He's been studying it in the club. He's always there.

CUTHBERTSON (*warmly*). Not always. Don't exaggerate, Charteris. You know very well that though I joined the club on Grace's account, thinking that her father's presence there would be a protection and a—a sort of sanction, as it were—I never approved of it.

CRAVEN (*tactlessly harping on Cuthbertson's inconsistency*). Well, you know, this is unexpected: now it's really very unexpected. I should never have thought it from hearing you talk, Jo. Why, you said the whole modern movement was abhorrent to you because your life had been passed in witnessing scenes of suffering nobly endured and sacrifice willingly rendered by womanly women and manly men and deuce knows what else. Is it at the Ibsen club that you see all this manliness and womanliness?

CHARTERIS. Certainly not: the rules of the club forbid anything of that sort. Every candidate for membership must be nominated by a man and a woman, who both guarantee that the candidate, if female, is not womanly, and if male, is not manly.

CRAVEN (*chuckling cunningly and stooping to press his heated trousers against his legs, which are chilly*). Won't do, Charteris. Can't take me in with so thin a story as that.

CUTHBERTSON (*vehemently*). It's true. It's monstrous, but it's true.

CRAVEN (*with rising indignation, as he begins to draw the inevitable inferences*). Do you mean to say that somebody had the audacity to guarantee that my Julia is not a womanly woman?

CHARTERIS (*darkly*). It sounds incredible; but a man was found ready to take that inconceivable lie on his conscience.

JULIA (*firing up*). If he has nothing worse than that on his conscience, he may sleep pretty well. In what way am I more womanly than any of the rest of them, I should like to know? They are always saying things like that behind my back—I hear of them from Sylvia. Only the other day a member of the committee said I ought never to have been elected—that you (*to Charteris*) had smuggled me in. I should like to see her say it to my face: that's all.

CRAVEN. But, my precious, I most sincerely hope she was right. She paid you the highest compliment. Why, the place must be a den of infamy.

CUTHBERTSON (*emphatically*). So it is, Craven, so it is.

CHARTERIS. Exactly. That's what keeps it so select: nobody but people whose reputations are above suspicion dare belong to it. If we once got a good name, we should become a mere whitewashing shop for all the shady characters in London. Better join us, Craven. Let me put you up.

CRAVEN. What! Join a club where there's some scoundrel who guaranteed my daughter to be an unwomanly woman! If I weren't an invalid, I'd kick him.

CHARTERIS. Oh don't say that. It was I who did it.

CRAVEN (*reproachfully*). You! Now upon my soul, Charteris, this is very vexing. Now how could you bring yourself to do such a thing?

CHARTERIS. She made me. Why, I had to guarantee Cuthbertson as unmanly; and he's the leading representative of manly sentiment in London.

CRAVEN. That didn't do Jo any harm: but it took away my Julia's character.

JULIA (*outraged*). Daddy!

CHARTERIS. Not at the Ibsen club, quite the contrary. After all, what can we do? You know what breaks up most clubs for men and women. There's a quarrel— a scandal—cherchez la femme—always a woman at the bottom of it. Well, we knew this when we founded the club; but we noticed that the woman at the bottom of it was always a womanly woman. The unwomanly women who work for their living and know how to take care of themselves never give any trouble. So we simply said we wouldn't have any womanly women; and when one gets smuggled in she has to take care not to behave in a womanly way. We get on all right. (*He rises.*) Come to lunch with me there tomorrow and see the place.

CUTHBERTSON (*rising*). No, he's engaged to me. But you can join us.

CHARTERIS. What hour?

CUTHBERTSON. Any time after twelve. (*To Craven*) It's at 90 Cork street, at the other end of the Burlington Arcade.

CRAVEN (*making a note*). 90, you say. After twelve. (*He suddenly relapses into gloom.*) By the bye, don't order anything special for me. I'm not allowed wine— only Apollinaris. No meat either—only a scrap of fish occasionally. I'm to have a short life, but not a merry one. (*Sighing.*) Well, well. (*Bracing himself up.*) Now, Julia, it's time for us to be off. (*Julia rises.*)

CUTHBERTSON. But where on earth is Grace? I must go and look for her. (*He turns to the door.*)

JULIA (*stopping him*). Oh, pray don't disturb her, Mr. Cuthbertson. She's so tired.

CUTHBERTSON. But just for a moment to say good night. (*Julia and Charteris look at one another in dismay. Cuthbertson looks quickly at them, perceiving that something is wrong.*)

CHARTERIS. We must make a clean breast of it, I see.

CUTHBERTSON. Clean breast?

CHARTERIS. The truth is, Cuthbertson, Mrs. Tranfield, who is, as you know, the most thoughtful of women, took it into her head that I—well, that I particularly wanted to speak to Miss Craven alone. So she said she was tired and wanted to go to bed.

CRAVEN (*scandalized*). Tut! tut!

CUTHBERTSON. Oho! is that it? Then it's all right. She never goes to bed as early as this. I'll fetch her in a moment. (*He goes out confidently, leaving Charteris aghast.*)

JULIA. Now you've done it. (*She rushes to the round table and snatches up her mantle and bonnet.*) I'm off. (*She makes for the door.*)

CRAVEN (*horrified*). What are you doing, Julia? You can't go until you've said good night to Mrs. Tranfield. It would be horribly rude.

JULIA. You can stay if you like, Daddy: I can't. I'll wait for you in the hall. (*She hurries out.*)

CRAVEN (*following her*). But what on earth am I to say? (*Stopping as she disappears, and turning to Charteris grumbling*) Now really you know, Charteris, this is devilish awkward, upon my life it is. That was a most indelicate thing of you to say plump out before us all—that about you and Julia.

CHARTERIS. I'll explain it all to-morrow. Just at present we'd really better follow Julia's example and bolt. (*He starts for the door.*)

CRAVEN (*intercepting him*). Stop! don't leave me like this: I shall look like a fool. Now I shall really take it in bad part if you run away, Charteris.

CHARTERIS (*resignedly*). All right. I'll stay. (*Lifts himself on to the shoulder of the grand piano and sits there swinging his legs and contemplating Craven resignedly.*)

CRAVEN (*pacing up and down*). I'm excessively vexed about Julia's conduct, I am indeed. She can't bear to be crossed in the slightest thing, poor child. I'll have to apologize for her you know: her going away is a downright slap in the face for these people here. Cuthbertson may be offended already for all I know.

CHARTERIS. Oh never mind about him. Mrs. Tranfield bosses this establishment.

CRAVEN (*cunningly*). Ah, that's it, is it? He's just the sort of fellow that would have no control over his daughter. (*He goes back to his former place on the hearthrug with his back to the fire.*) By the bye, what the dickens did he mean by all that about passing his life amid—what was it?—" scenes of suffering nobly endured and sacrifice willingly rendered by womanly women and manly men" and a lot more of the same sort? I suppose he's something in a hospital.

CHARTERIS. Hospital! Nonsense: he's a dramatic critic. Didn't you hear me say that he was the leading representative of manly sentiment in London?

CRAVEN. You don't say so. Now really, who'd have thought it! How jolly it must be to be able to go to the theatre for nothing! I must ask him to get me a few tickets occasionally. But isn't it ridiculous for a man to talk like that! I'm hanged if he don't take what he sees on the stage quite seriously.

CHARTERIS. Of course: that's why he's a good critic. Besides, if you take people seriously off the stage, why shouldn't you take them seriously on it, where they're under some sort of decent restraint? (*He jumps down off piano and goes up to the window. Cuthbertson comes back.*)

CUTHBERTSON (*to Craven, rather sheepishly*). The fact is, Grace has gone to bed. I must apologize to you and Miss— (*He turns to Julia's seat, and stops on seeing it vacant.*)

CRAVEN (*embarrassed*). It is I who have to apologize for Julia, Jo. She—

CHARTERIS (*interrupting*). She said she was quite sure that if we didn't go, you'd persuade Mrs. Tranfield to get up to say good night for the sake of politeness; so she went straight off.

CUTHBERTSON. Very kind of her indeed. I'm really ashamed—

CRAVEN. Don't mention it, Jo, don't mention it. She's waiting for me below. *(Going.)* Good night. Good night, Charteris.

CHARTERIS. Good night.

CUTHBERTSON *(seeing Craven out)*. Goodnight. Say good night and thanks to Miss Craven for me. To-morrow any time after twelve, remember. *(They go out; and Charteris with a long sigh crosses to the fireplace, thoroughly tired out.)*

CRAVEN *(outside)*. All right.

CUTHBERTSON *(outside)*. Take care of the stairs; they're rather steep. Good night. *(The outside door shuts; and Cuthbertson returns. Instead of entering, he stands in the doorway with one hand in the breast of his waistcoat, eyeing Charteris sternly.)*

CHARTERIS. What's the matter?

CUTHBERTSON *(sternly)*. Charteris: what's been going on here? I insist on knowing. Grace has not gone to bed: I have seen and spoken with her. What is it all about?

CHARTERIS. Ask your theatrical experience, Cuthbertson. A man, of course.

CUTHBERTSON *(coming forward and confronting him)*. Don't play the fool with me, Charteris: I'm too old a hand to be amused by it. I ask you, seriously, what's the matter?

CHARTERIS. I tell you, seriously, I'm the matter, Julia wants to marry me: I want to marry Grace. I came here to-night to sweetheart Grace. Enter Julia. Alarums and excursions. Exit Grace. Enter you and Craven. Subterfuges and excuses. Exeunt Craven and Julia. And here we are. That's the whole story. Sleep over it. Good night. *(He leaves.)*

CUTHBERTSON *(staring after him)*. Well I'll be— (The act drop descends.)

END OF ACT I.

ACT II

NEXT day at noon, in the Library of the Ibsen club. A spacious room, with glass doors right and left. At the back, in the middle, is the fireplace, surmounted by a handsome mantelpiece, with a bust of Ibsen, and decorated inscriptions of the titles of his plays. There are circular recesses at each side of fireplace, with divan seats running round them, and windows at the top, the space between the divan and the window sills being lined with books. A long settee is placed before the fire. Along the back of the settee, and touching it, is a green table, littered with journals. A revolving bookcase stands in the foreground, a little to the left, with an easy chair close to it. On the right, between the door and the recess, is a light library stepladder. Placards inscribed "silence" are conspicuously exhibited here and there.

(Cuthbertson is seated in the easy chair at the revolving bookstand, reading the "Daily Graphic." Dr. Paramore is on the divan in the right hand recess, reading "The British Medical Journal." He is young as age is counted in the professions—barely forty. His hair is wearing bald on his forehead; and his dark arched eyebrows, coming rather close together, give him a conscientiously sinister appearance. He wears the frock coat and cultivates the "bedside manner" of the fashionable physician with scrupulous conventionality. Not at all a happy or frank man, but not consciously unhappy nor intentionally insincere, and highly self satisfied intellectually.

Sylvia Craven is sitting in the middle of the settee before the fire, only the back of her head being visible. She is reading a volume of Ibsen. She is a girl of eighteen, small and trim, wearing a smart tailor-made dress, rather short, and a Newmarket jacket, showing a white blouse with a light silk sash and a man's collar and watch chain so arranged as to look as like a man's waistcoat and shirt-front as possible without spoiling the prettiness of the effect. A Page Boy's voice, monotonously calling for Dr. Paramore, is heard approaching outside on the right.)

PAGE (outside). Dr. Paramore, Dr. Paramore, Dr. Paramore. (He enters carrying a salver with a card on it.) Dr. Par—

PARAMORE (sharply, sitting up). Here, boy. (The boy presents the salver. Paramore takes the card and looks at it.) All right: I'll come down to him. (The boy goes. Paramore rises, and comes from the recess, throwing his paper on the table.) Good morning, Mr. Cuthbertson (stopping to pull out his cuffs and shake his coat straight) Mrs. Tranfield quite well, I hope?

SYLVIA (turning her head indignantly). Sh—sh—sh! (Paramore turns, surprised. Cuthbertson rises energetically and looks across the bookstand to see who is the author of this impertinence.)

PARAMORE (to Sylvia—stiffly). I beg your pardon, Miss Craven: I did not mean to disturb you.

SYLVIA (flustered and self assertive). You may talk as much as you like if you will only have the common consideration to first ask whether the other people object. What I protest against is your assumption that my presence doesn't matter because I'm only a female member. That's all. Now go on, pray: you don't disturb me in the least. *(She turns to the fire, and again buries herself in Ibsen.)*

CUTHBERTSON *(with emphatic dignity)*. No gentleman would have dreamt of objecting to our exchanging a few words, madam. *(She takes no notice. He resumes angrily.)* As a matter of fact I was about to say to Dr. Paramore that if he would care to bring his visitor up here, *I* should not object. The impudence! *(Dashes his paper down on the chair.)*

PARAMORE. Oh, many thanks; but it's only an instrument maker.

CUTHBERTSON. Any new medical discoveries, doctor?

PARAMORE. Well, since you ask me, yes—perhaps a most important one. I have discovered something that has hitherto been overlooked—a minute duct in the liver of the guinea pig. Miss Craven will forgive my mentioning it when I say that it may throw an important light on her father's case. The first thing, of course, is to find out what the duct is there for.

CUTHBERTSON *(reverently—feeling that he is in the presence of science)*. Indeed. How will you do that?

PARAMORE. Oh, easily enough, by simply cutting the duct and seeing what will happen to the guinea pig. *(Sylvia rises, horrified.)* I shall require a knife specially made to get at it. The man who is waiting for me downstairs has brought me a few handles to try before fitting it and sending it to the laboratory. I am afraid it would not do to bring such weapons up here.

SYLVIA. If you attempt such a thing, Dr. Paramore, I will complain to the committee. The majority of the committee are anti-vivisectionists. You ought to be ashamed of yourself. *(She flounces out at the right hand door.)*

PARAMORE *(with patient contempt)*. That's the sort of thing we scientific men have to put up with nowadays, Mr. Cuthbertson. Ignorance, superstition, sentimentality: they are all one. A guinea pig's convenience is set above the health and lives of the entire human race.

CUTHBERTSON *(vehemently)*. It's not ignorance or superstition, Paramore: it's sheer downright Ibsenism: that's what it is. I've been wanting to sit comfortably at the fire the whole morning; but I've never had a chance with that girl there. I couldn't go and plump myself down on a seat beside her: goodness knows what she'd think I wanted. That's one of the delights of having women in the club: when they come in here they all want to sit at the fire and adore that bust. I sometimes feel that I should like to take the poker and fetch it a wipe across the nose—ugh!

PARAMORE. I must say I prefer the elder Miss Craven to her sister.

CUTHBERTSON *(his eyes lighting up)*. Ah, Julia! I believe you. A splendid fine creature—every inch a woman. No Ibsenism about her!

PARAMORE. I quite agree with you there, Mr. Cuthbertson. Er—by the way, do you think is Miss Craven attached to Charteris at all?

CUTHBERTSON. What, that fellow! Not he. He hangs about after her; but he's not man enough for her. A woman of that sort likes a strong, manly, deep-throated, broad-chested man.

PARAMORE *(anxiously)*. Hm, a sort of sporting character, you think?

CUTHBERTSON. Oh, no, no. A scientific man, perhaps, like yourself. But you know what I mean—a MAN. *(Strikes himself a sounding blow on the chest.)*

PARAMORE. Of course; but Charteris is a man.

CUTHBERTSON. Pah! you don't see what I mean. *(The Page Boy returns with his salver.)*

PAGE BOY *(calling monotonously as before)*. Mr. Cuthbertson, Mr. Cuthbertson, Mr. Cuth—

CUTHBERTSON. Here, boy. *(He takes a card from the salver.)* Bring the gentleman up here. *(The boy goes out.)* It's Craven. He's coming to lunch with me and Charteris. You might join us if you've nothing better to do, when you've finished with the instrument man. If Julia turns up I'll ask her too.

PARAMORE *(flushing with pleasure)*. I shall be very happy. Thank you. *(He is going out at the right hand door when Craven enters.)* Good morning, Colonel Craven.

CRAVEN *(at the door)*. Good morning—glad to see you. I'm looking for Cuthbertson.

PARAMORE *(smiling)*. There he is. *(He goes out.)*

CUTHBERTSON *(greeting Craven effusively)*. Delighted to see you. Now will you come to the smoking room, or will you sit down here and have a chat while we're waiting for Charteris. If you like company, the smoking room is always full of women. Here we shall have it pretty well all to ourselves until about three o'clock.

CRAVEN. I don't like to see women smoking. I'll make myself comfortable here. *(Sits in an easy chair on the right.)*

CUTHBERTSON *(taking a chair beside him, on his left)*. Neither do I. There's not a room in this club where I can enjoy a pipe quietly without a woman coming in and beginning to roll a cigarette. It's a disgusting habit in a woman: it's not natural to her sex.

CRAVEN *(sighing)*. Ah, Jo, times have changed since we both courted Molly Ebden all those years ago. I took my defeat well, old chap, didn't I?

CUTHBERTSON *(with earnest approval)*. You did, Dan. The thought of it has often helped me to behave well myself: it has, on my honour.

CRAVEN. Yes, you always believe in hearth and home, Jo—in a true English wife and a happy wholesome fireside. How did Molly turn out?

CUTHBERTSON *(trying to be fair to Molly)*. Well, not bad. She might have been worse. You see I couldn't stand her relations: all the men were roaring cads; and she couldn't get on with my mother. And then she hated being in town; and of course I couldn't live in the country on account of my work. But we hit it off as well as most people, until we separated.

CRAVEN *(taken aback)*. Separated! *(He is irresistibly amused.)* Oh, that was the end of the hearth and home, Jo, was it?

CUTHBERTSON *(warmly)*. It was not my fault, Dan. *(Sentimentally.)* Some day the world will know how I loved that woman. But she was incapable of valuing a true man's affection. Do you know, she often said she wished she'd married you instead.

CRAVEN (sobered by the suggestion). Dear me, dear me! Well, perhaps it was better as it was. You heard about my marriage, I suppose.

CUTHBERTSON. Oh yes: we all heard of it.

CRAVEN. Well, Jo, I may as well make a clean breast of it—everybody knew it. I married for money.

CUTHBERTSON (encouragingly). And why not, Dan, why not? We can't get on without it, you know.

CRAVEN (with sincere feeling). I got to be very fond of her, Jo. I had a home until she died. Now everything's changed. Julia's always here. Sylvia's of a different nature; but she's always here too.

CUTHBERTSON (sympathetically). I know. It's the same with Grace. She's always here.

CRAVEN. And now they want me to be always here. They're at me every day to join the club—to stop my grumbling, I suppose. That's what I want to consult you about. Do you think I ought to join?

CUTHBERTSON. Well, if you have no conscientious objection—

CRAVEN (testily interrupting him). I object to the existence of the place on principle; but what's the use of that? Here it is in spite of my objection, and I may as well have the benefit of any good that may be in it.

CUTHBERTSON (soothing him). Of course: that's the only reasonable view of the matter. Well, the fact is, it's not so inconvenient as you might think. When you're at home, you have the house more to yourself; and when you want to have your family about you, you can dine with them at the club.

CRAVEN (not much attracted by this). True.

CUTHBERTSON. Besides, if you don't want to dine with them, you needn't.

CRAVEN (convinced). True, very true. But don't they carry on here, rather?

CUTHBERTSON. Oh, no, they don't exactly carry on. Of course the usual tone of the club is low, because the women smoke and earn their own living and all that; but still there's nothing actually to complain of. And it's convenient, certainly. (Charteris comes in, looking round for them.)

CRAVEN (rising). Do you know, I've a great mind to join, just to see what it's like. Would you mind putting me up?

CUTHBERTSON. Delighted, Dan, delighted. (He grasps Craven's hand.)

CHARTERIS (putting one hand on Craven's shoulder and the other on Cuthbertson's). Bless you, my children! (Cuthbertson, a little wounded in his dignity, moves away. The Colonel takes the jest in the utmost good humor.)

CRAVEN (cordially). Hallo!

CHARTERIS (to Craven). Hope I haven't disturbed your chat by coming too soon.

CRAVEN. Not at all. Welcome, dear boy. (Shakes his hand.)

CHARTERIS. That's right. I'm earlier than I intended. The fact is, I have something rather pressing to say to Cuthbertson.

CRAVEN. Private!

CHARTERIS. Not particularly. (To Cuthbertson.) Only what we were speaking of last night.

CUTHBERTSON. Well, Charteris, I think that is private, or ought to be.

CRAVEN (*going up towards the table*). I'll just take a look at the Times—

CHARTERIS (*stopping him*). Oh, it's no secret: everybody in the club guesses it. (*To Cuthbertson.*) Has Grace never mentioned to you that she wants to marry me?

CUTHBERTSON (*indignantly*). She has mentioned that you want to marry her.

CHARTERIS. Ah; but then it's not what I want, but what Grace wants, that will weigh with you.

CRAVEN (*a little shocked*). Excuse me Charteris: this is private. I'll leave you to yourselves. (*Again moves towards the table.*)

CHARTERIS. Wait a bit, Craven: you're concerned in this. Julia wants to marry me too.

CRAVEN (*in a tone of the strongest remonstrance*). Now really! Now upon my life and soul!

CHARTERIS. It's a fact, I assure you. Didn't it strike you as rather odd, our being up there last night and Mrs. Tranfield not with us?

CRAVEN. Well, yes it did. But you explained it. And now really, Charteris, I must say your explanation was in shocking bad taste before Julia.

CHARTERIS. Never mind. It was a good, fat, healthy, bouncing lie.

CRAVEN and CUTHBERTSON. Lie!

CHARTERIS. Didn't you suspect that?

CRAVEN. Certainly not. Did you, Jo?

CUTHBERTSON. No, most emphatically.

CRAVEN. What's more, I don't believe you. I'm sorry to have to say such a thing; but you forget that Julia was present and didn't contradict you.

CHARTERIS. She didn't want to.

CRAVEN. Do you mean to say that my daughter deceived me?

CHARTERIS. Delicacy towards me compelled her to, Craven.

CRAVEN (*taking a very serious tone*). Now look here, Charteris: have you any proper sense of the fact that you're standing between two fathers?

CUTHBERTSON. Quite right, Dan, quite right. I repeat the question on my own account.

CHARTERIS. Well, I'm a little dazed still by standing for so long between two daughters; but I think I grasp the situation. (*Cuthbertson flings away with an exclamation of disgust.*)

CRAVEN. Then I'm sorry for your manners, Charteris: that's all. (*He turns away sulkily; then suddenly fires up and turns on Charteris.*) How dare you tell me my daughter wants to marry you. Who are you, pray, that she should have any such ambition?

CHARTERIS. Just so; she couldn't have made a worse choice. But she won't listen to reason. I've talked to her like a father myself—I assure you, my dear Craven, I've said everything that you could have said; but it's no use: she won't give me up. And if she won't listen to me, what likelihood is there of her listening to you?

CRAVEN (*in angry bewilderment*). Cuthbertson: did you ever hear anything like this?

CUTHBERTSON. Never! Never!

CHARTERIS. Oh, bother? Come, don't behave like a couple of conventional old fathers: this is a serious affair. Look at these letters (*producing a letter and a letter-card.*) This (*showing the card*) is from Grace—by the way, Cuthbertson, I wish you'd ask her not to write on letter-cards: the blue colour makes it so easy for Julia to pick the bits out of my waste paper basket and piece them together. Now listen. "My dear Leonard: Nothing could make it worth my while to be exposed to such scenes as last night's. You had much better go back to Julia and forget me. Yours sincerely, Grace Tranfield."

CUTHBERTSON (*infuriated*). Damnation!

CHARTERIS (*turning to Craven and preparing to read the letter*). Now for Julia. (*The Colonel turns away to hide his face from Charteris, anticipating a shock, and puts his hand on a chair to steady himself.*) "My dearest boy. Nothing will make me believe that this odious woman can take my place in your heart. I send some of the letters you wrote me when we first met; and I ask you to read them. They will recall what you felt when you wrote them. You cannot have changed so much as to be indifferent to me: whoever may have struck your fancy for the moment, your heart is still mine"—and so on: you know the sort of thing—"Ever and always your loving Julia." (*The Colonel sinks on the chair and covers his face with his hand.*) You don't suppose she's serious, do you: that's the sort of thing she writes me three times a day. (*To Cuthbertson*) Grace is in earnest though, confound it. (*He holds out Grace's letter.*) A blue card as usual! This time I shall not trust the waste paper basket. (*He goes to the fire, and throws the letters into it.*)

CUTHBERTSON (*facing him with folded arms as he comes down again*). May I ask, Mr. Charteris, is this the New Humour?

CHARTERIS (*still too preoccupied with his own difficulty to have any sense of the effect he is producing on the others*). Oh, stuff! Do you suppose it's a joke to be situated as I am? You've got your head so stuffed with the New Humour and the New Woman and the New This, That and the Other, all mixed up with your own old Adam, that you've lost your senses.

CUTHBERTSON (*strenuously*). Do you see that old man, grown grey in the honoured service of his country, whose last days you have blighted?

CHARTERIS (*surprised, looking at Craven and realizing his distress with genuine concern*). I'm very sorry. Come, Craven; don't take it to heart. (*Craven shakes his head.*) I assure you it means nothing: it happens to me constantly.

CUTHBERTSON. There is only one excuse for you. You are not fully responsible for your actions. Like all advanced people, you have got neurasthenia.

CHARTERIS (*appalled*). Great Heavens! what's that?

CUTHBERTSON. I decline to explain. You know as well as I do. I am going downstairs now to order lunch. I shall order it for three; but the third place is for Paramore, whom I have invited, not for you. (*He goes out through the left hand door.)*

CHARTERIS *(putting his hand on Craven's shoulder).* Come, Craven; advise me. You've been in this sort of fix yourself probably.

CRAVEN. Charteris: no woman writes such letters to a man unless he has made advances to her.

CHARTERIS *(mournfully).* How little you know the world, Colonel! The New Woman is not like that.

CRAVEN. I can only give you very old fashioned advice, my boy; and that is that it's well to be off with the Old Woman before you're on with the New. I'm sorry you told me. You might have waited for my death: it's not far off now. *(His head droops again. Julia and Paramore enter on the right. Julia stops as she catches sight of Charteris, her face clouding and her breast heaving. Paramore, seeing the Colonel apparently ill, hurries down to him with the bedside manner in full play.)*

CHARTERIS *(seeing Julia).* Oh Lord! *(He retreats under the lee of the revolving bookstand.)*

PARAMORE *(sympathetically to the Colonel).* Allow me. *(Takes his wrist and begins to count his pulse.)*

CRAVEN *(looking up).* Eh? *(Withdraws his hand and rises rather crossly.)* No, Paramore: it's not my liver now: it's private business. *(A chase now begins between Julia and Charteris, all the more exciting to them because the huntress and her prey must alike conceal the real object of their movements from the others. Charteris first makes for the right hand door. Julia immediately moves back to it, barring his path. He doubles back round the bookstand, setting it whirling as he makes for the left door, Julia crossing in pursuit of him. He is about to escape when he is cut off by the return of Cuthbertson. He turns back and sees Julia close upon him. There being nothing else for it, he bolts up into the recess to the left of the fireplace.)*

CUTHBERTSON. Good morning, Miss Craven. *(They shake hands.)* Won't you join us at lunch? Paramore's coming too.

JULIA. Thanks: I shall be very pleased. *(She goes up with affected purposelessness towards the recess. Charteris, almost trapped in it, crosses to the right hand recess by way of the fender, knocking down the fire irons with a crash as he does so.)*

CRAVEN *(who has crossed to the whirling bookcase and stopped it).* What the dickens are you doing there, Charteris?

CHARTERIS. Nothing. It's such a confounded room to get about in.

JULIA *(maliciously).* Yes, isn't it. *(She is moving back to guard the right hand door, when Cuthbertson appears at it.)*

CUTHBERTSON. May I take you down? *(He offers her his arm.)*

JULIA. No, really: you know it's against the rules of the club to coddle women in any way. Whoever is nearest to the door goes first.

CUTHBERTSON. Oh well, if you insist. Come, gentlemen: let us go to lunch in the Ibsen fashion—the unsexed fashion. *(He goes out on the left followed by Paramore, laughing. Craven goes last. He turns at the door to see whether Julia is coming, and stops when he sees she is not.)*

CRAVEN. Come, Julia.

JULIA *(with patronising affection).* Yes, Daddy, dear, presently. *(Charteris is meanwhile stealing to the right hand door.)* Don't wait for me: I'll come in a moment. *(The Colonel hesitates.)* It's all right, Daddy.

CRAVEN *(very gravely)*. Don't be long, my dear. *(He goes out.)*

CHARTERIS. I'm off. *(Makes a dash for the right hand door.)*

JULIA *(darting at him and seizing his wrist)*. Aren't you coming?

CHARTERIS. No. Unhand me Julia. *(He tries to get away: she holds him.)* If you don't let me go, I'll scream for help.

JULIA *(reproachfully)*. Leonard! *(He breaks away from her.)* Oh, how can you be so rough with me, dear. Did you get my letter?

CHARTERIS. Burnt it—*(she turns away, struck to the heart, and buries her face in her hands)*—along with hers.

JULIA *(quickly turning again)*. Hers! Has she written to you?

CHARTERIS. Yes, to break off with me on your account.

JULIA *(her eyes gleaming)*. Ah!

CHARTERIS. You are pleased. Wretch! Now you have lost the last scrap of my regard. *(He turns to go, but is stopped by the return of Sylvia. Julia turns away and stands pretending to read a paper which she picks up from the table.)*

SYLVIA *(offhandedly)*. Hallo, Charteris: how are you getting on? *(She takes his arm familiarly and walks down the room with him.)* Have you seen Grace Tranfield this morning? *(Julia drops the paper and comes a step nearer to listen.)* You generally know where she is to be found.

CHARTERIS. I shall never know any more, Sylvia. She's quarrelled with me.

SYLVIA. Sylvia! How often am I to tell you that I am not Sylvia at the club?

CHARTERIS. I forgot. I beg your pardon, Craven, old chap *(slaps her on the shoulder)*.

SYLVIA. That's better—a little overdone, but better.

JULIA. Don't be a fool, Silly.

SYLVIA. Remember, Julia, if you please, that here we are members of the club, not sisters. I don't take liberties with you here on family grounds: don't you take any with me. *(She goes to the settee and resumes her former place.)*

CHARTERIS. Quite right, Craven. Down with the tyranny of the elder sister!

JULIA. You ought to know better than to encourage a child to make herself ridiculous, Leonard, even at my expense.

CHARTERIS *(seating himself on the edge of the table)*. Your lunch will be cold, Julia. *(Julia is about to retort furiously when she is checked by the reappearance of Cuthbertson at the left hand door.)*

CUTHBERTSON. What has become of you, Miss Craven? Your father is getting quite uneasy. We're all waiting for you.

JULIA. So I have just been reminded, thank you. *(She goes out angrily past him, Sylvia looking round to see.)*

CUTHBERTSON *(looking first after her, then at Charteris)*. More neurasthenia. *(He follows her.)*

SYLVIA *(jumping up on her knees on the settee and speaking over the back of it)*.

What's up, Charteris? Julia been making love to you?

CHARTERIS *(speaking to her over his shoulder)*. No. Blowing me up for making love to Grace.

SYLVIA. Serve you right. You are an awful devil for philandering.

CHARTERIS *(calmly)*. Do you consider it good club form to talk that way to a man who might nearly be your father?

SYLVIA *(knowingly)*. Oh, I know you, my lad.

CHARTERIS. Then you know that I never pay any special attention to any woman.

SYLVIA *(thoughtfully)*. Do you know, Leonard, I really believe you. I don't think you care a bit more for one woman than for another.

CHARTERIS. You mean I don't care a bit less for one woman than another.

SYLVIA. That makes it worse. But what I mean is that you never bother about their being only women: you talk to them just as you do to me or any other fellow. That's the secret of your success. You can't think how sick they get of being treated with the respect due to their sex.

CHARTERIS. Ah, if Julia only had your wisdom, Craven! *(He gets off the table with a sigh and perches himself reflectively on the stepladder.)*

SYLVIA. She can't take things easy, can she, old man? But don't you be afraid of breaking her heart: she gets over her little tragedies. We found that out at home when our great sorrow came.

CHARTERIS. What was that?

SYLVIA. I mean when we learned that poor papa had Paramore's disease. But it was too late to inoculate papa. All they could do was to prolong his life for two years more by putting him on a strict diet. Poor old boy! they cut off his liquor; and he's not allowed to eat meat.

CHARTERIS. Your father appears to me to be uncommonly well.

SYLVIA. Yes, you would think he was a great deal better. But the microbes are at work, slowly but surely. In another year it will be all over. Poor old Dad! it's unfeeling to talk about him in this attitude: I must sit down properly. *(She comes down from the settee and takes the chair near the bookstand.)* I should like papa to live for ever just to take the conceit out of Paramore. I believe he's in love with Julia.

CHARTERIS *(starting up excitedly)*. In love with Julia! A ray of hope on the horizon! Do you really mean it?

SYLVIA. I should think I do. Why do you suppose he's hanging about the club to-day in a beautiful new coat and tie instead of attending to his patients? That lunch with Julia will finish him. He'll ask Daddy's consent before they come back—I'll bet you three to one he will, in anything you please.

CHARTERIS. Gloves?

SYLVIA. No: cigarettes.

CHARTERIS. Done! But what does she think about it? Does she give him any encouragement?

SYLVIA. Oh, the usual thing. Enough to keep any other woman from getting him.

CHARTERIS. Just so. I understand. Now listen to me: I am going to speak as a philosopher. Julia is jealous of everybody—everybody. If she saw you flirting with Paramore she'd begin to value him directly. You might play up a little, Craven, for my sake—eh?

SYLVIA (*rising*). You're too awful, Leonard. For shame? However, anything to oblige a fellow Ibsenite. I'll bear your affair in mind. But I think it would be more effective if you got Grace to do it.

CHARTERIS. Think so? Hm! perhaps you're right.

PAGE BOY (*outside as before*). Dr. Paramore, Dr. Paramore, Dr. Paramore—

SYLVIA. They ought to get that boy's voice properly cultivated: it's a disgrace to the club. (*She goes into the recess on Ibsen's left. The page enters carrying the British Medical Journal.*)

CHARTERIS (*calling to the page*). Dr. Paramore is in the dining room.

PAGE BOY. Thank you, sir. (*He is about to go into the dining room when Sylvia swoops on him.*)

SYLVIA. Here: where are you taking that paper? It belongs to this room.

PAGE BOY. It's Dr. Paramore's particular orders, miss. The British Medical Journal has always to be brought to him dreckly it comes.

SYLVIA. What cheek? Charteris: oughtn't we to stop this on principle?

CHARTERIS. Certainly not. Principle's the poorest reason I know for making yourself nasty.

SYLVIA. Bosh! Ibsen!

CHARTERIS (*to the page*). Off with you, my boy: Dr. Paramore's waiting breathless with expectation.

PAGE BOY (*seriously*). Indeed, sir. (*He hurries off.*)

CHARTERIS. That boy will make his way in this country. He has no sense of humour. (*Grace comes in. Her dress, very convenient and businesslike, is made to please herself and serve her own purposes without the slightest regard to fashion, though by no means without a careful concern for her personal elegance. She enters briskly, like an habitually busy woman.*)

SYLVIA (*running to her*). Here you are at last Tranfield, old girl. I've been waiting for you this last hour. I'm starving.

GRACE. All right, dear. (*To Charteris.*) Did you get my letter?

CHARTERIS. Yes. I wish you wouldn't write on those confounded blue letter cards.

SYLVIA (*to Grace*). Shall I go down first and secure a table?

CHARTERIS (*taking the reply out of Grace's mouth*). Do, old boy.

SYLVIA. Don't be too long. (*She goes into the dining room.*)

GRACE. Well?

CHARTERIS. I'm afraid to face you after last night. Can you imagine a more horrible scene? Don't you hate the very sight of me after it?

GRACE. Oh, no.

CHARTERIS. Then you ought to. Ugh! it was hideous—an insult—an outrage. A nice end to all my plans for making you happy—for making you an exception to all the women who swear I have made them miserable!

GRACE *(sitting down placidly)*. I am not at all miserable. I'm sorry; but I shan't break my heart.

CHARTERIS. No: yours is a thoroughbred heart: you don't scream and cry every time it's pinched. That's why you are the only possible woman for me.

GRACE *(shaking her head)*. Not now. Never any more.

CHARTERIS. Never! What do you mean?

GRACE. What I say, Leonard.

CHARTERIS. Jilted again! The fickleness of women I love is only equaled by the infernal constancy of the women who love me. Well, well! I see how it is, Grace: you can't get over that horrible scene last night. Imagine her saying I had kissed her within the last two days!

GRACE *(rising eagerly)*. Was that not true?

CHARTERIS. True! No: a thumping lie.

GRACE. Oh, I'm so glad. That was the only thing that really hurt me.

CHARTERIS. Just why she said it. How adorable of you to care! My darling. *(He seizes her hands and presses them to his breast.)*

GRACE. Remember! it's all broken off.

CHARTERIS. Ah yes: you have my heart in your hands. Break it. Throw my happiness out of the window.

GRACE. Oh, Leonard, does your happiness really depend on me?

CHARTERIS *(tenderly)*. Absolutely. *(She beams with delight. A sudden revulsion comes to him at the sight: he recoils, dropping her hands and crying)* Ah no: why should I lie to you? *(He folds his arms and adds firmly)* My happiness depends on nobody but myself. I can do without you.

GRACE *(nerving herself)*. So you shall. Thank you for the truth. Now *I* will tell you the truth.

CHARTERIS *(unfolding his arms and again recoiling)*. No, please. Don't. As a philosopher, it's my business to tell other people the truth; but it's not their business to tell it to me. I don't like it: it hurts.

GRACE *(quietly)*. It's only that I love you.

CHARTERIS. Ah! that's not a philosophic truth. You may tell me that as often as you like. *(He takes her in his arms.)*

GRACE. Yes, Leonard; but I'm an advanced woman. *(He checks himself and looks at her in some consternation.)* I'm what my father calls a New Woman. *(He lets her go and stares at her.)* I quite agree with all your ideas.

CHARTERIS *(scandalized)*. That's a nice thing for a respectable woman to say! You ought to be ashamed of yourself.

GRACE. I am quite in earnest about them too, though you are not; and I will never marry a man I love too much. It would give him a terrible advantage over me: I should be utterly in his power. That's what the New Woman is like. Isn't she right, Mr. Philosopher?

CHARTERIS. The struggle between the Philosopher and the Man is fearful, Grace. But the Philosopher says you are right.

GRACE. I know I am right. And so we must part.

CHARTERIS. Not at all. You must marry some one else; and then I'll come and philander with you. *(Sylvia comes back.)*

SYLVIA *(holding the door open)*. Oh, I say: come along. I'm starving.

CHARTERIS. So am I. I'll lunch with you if I may.

SYLVIA. I thought you would. I've ordered soup for three. *(Grace passes out. Sylvia continues, to Charteris)* You can watch Paramore from our table: he's pretending to read the British Medical Journal; but he must be making up his mind for the plunge: he looks green with nervousness.

CHARTERIS. Good luck to him. *(He goes out, followed by Sylvia.)*

END OF ACT II.

ACT III

STILL the library. Ten minutes later. Julia, angry and miserable, comes in from the dining room, followed by Craven. She crosses the room tormentedly, and throws herself into a chair.

CRAVEN *(impatiently)*. What is the matter? Has everyone gone mad to-day? What do you mean by suddenly getting up from the table and tearing away like that? What does Paramore mean by reading his paper and not answering when he's spoken to? *(Julia writhes impatiently.)* Come, come *(tenderly)*: won't my pet tell her own father what— *(irritably)* what the devil is wrong with everybody? Do pull yourself straight, Julia, before Cuthbertson comes. He's only paying the bill: he'll be here in a moment.

JULIA. I couldn't bear it any longer. Oh, to see them sitting there at lunch together, laughing, chatting, making game of me! I should have screamed out in another moment—I should have taken a knife and killed her—I should have— *(Cuthbertson appears with the luncheon bill in his hand. He stuffs it into his waistcoat pocket as he comes to them. He begins speaking the moment he enters.)*

CUTHBERTSON. I'm afraid you've had a very poor lunch, Dan. It's disheartening to see you picking at a few beans and drinking soda water. I wonder how you live!

JULIA. That's all he ever takes, Mr. Cuthbertson, I assure you. He hates to be bothered about it.

CRAVEN. Where's Paramore?

CUTHBERTSON. Reading his paper, I asked him wasn't he coming; but he didn't hear me. It's amazing how anything scientific absorbs him. Clever man! Monstrously clever man!

CRAVEN *(pettishly)*. Oh yes, that's all very well, Jo; but it's not good manners at table: he should shut up the shop sometimes. Heaven knows I am only too anxious to forget his science, since it has pronounced my doom. *(He sits down with a melancholy air.)*

CUTHBERTSON *(compassionately)*. You mustn't think about that, Craven: perhaps he was mistaken. *(He sighs deeply and sits down.)* But he is certainly a very clever fellow. He thinks twice before he commits himself. *(They sit in silence, full of the gloomiest thoughts. Suddenly Paramore enters, pale and in the utmost disorder, with the British Medical Journal in his clenched hand. They rise in alarm. He tries to speak, but chokes, clutches at his throat, and staggers. Cuthbertson quickly takes his chair and places it behind Paramore, who sinks into it as they crowd about him, Craven at his right shoulder, Cuthbertson on his left, and Julia behind Craven.)*

CRAVEN. What's the matter, Paramore?

JULIA. Are you ill?

CUTHBERTSON. No bad news, I hope?

PARAMORE *(despairingly)*. The worst of news! Terrible news! Fatal news! My disease—

CRAVEN *(quickly)*. Do you mean my disease?

PARAMORE (*fiercely*). I mean my disease—Paramore's disease—the disease I discovered—the work of my life. Look here (*pointing to the B. M. J. with a ghastly expression of horror.*) If this is true, it was all a mistake: there is no such disease. (*Cuthbertson and Julia look at one another, hardly daring to believe the good news.*)

CRAVEN (*in strong remonstrance*). And you call this bad news! Now really, Paramore—

PARAMORE (*cutting him short hoarsely*). It's natural for you to think only of yourself. I don't blame you: all invalids are selfish. Only a scientific man can feel what I feel now. (*Writhing under a sense of intolerable injustice.*) It's the fault of the wickedly sentimental laws of this country. I was not able to make experiments enough—only three dogs and a monkey. Think of that, with all Europe full of my professional rivals—men burning to prove me wrong! There is freedom in France—enlightened republican France. One Frenchman experiments on two hundred monkeys to disprove my theory. Another sacrifices 36 pounds—three hundred dogs at three francs apiece—to upset the monkey experiments. A third proves them to be both wrong by a single experiment in which he gets the temperature of a camel's liver 60 degrees below zero. And now comes this cursed Italian who has ruined me. He has a government grant to buy animals with, besides the run of the largest hospital in Italy. (*With desperate resolution*) But I won't be beaten by any Italian. I'll go to Italy myself. I'll re-discover my disease: I know it exists; I feel it; and I'll prove it if I have to experiment on every mortal animal that's got a liver at all. (*He folds his arms and breathes hard at them.*)

CRAVEN (*his sense of injury growing upon him*). Am I to understand, Paramore, that you took it on yourself to pass sentence of death—yes, of Death—on me, on the strength of three dogs and an infernal monkey?

PARAMORE (*utterly contemptuous of Craven's narrow personal view of the matter*). Yes. That was all I could get a license for.

CRAVEN. Now upon my soul, Paramore, I'm vexed at this. I don't wish to be unfriendly; but I'm extremely vexed, really. Why, confound it, do you realize what you've done? You've cut off my meat and drink for a year—made me an object of public scorn—a miserable vegetarian and a teetotaller.

PARAMORE (*rising*). Well, you can make up for lost time now. (*Bitterly, shewing Craven the Journal*) There! you can read for yourself. The camel was fed on beef dissolved in alcohol; and he gained weight under it. Eat and drink as much as you please. (*Still unable to stand without support, he makes his way past Cuthbertson to the revolving bookcase and stands there with his back to them, leaning on it with his head on his hand.*)

CRAVEN (*grumbling*). Oh yes, it's very easy for you to talk, Paramore. But what am I to say to the Humanitarian societies and the Vegetarian societies that have made me a Vice President?

CUTHBERTSON (*chuckling*). Aha! You made a virtue of it, did you, Dan?

CRAVEN (*warmly*). I made a virtue of necessity, Jo. No one can blame me.

JULIA (*soothing him*). Well, never mind, Daddy. Come back to the dining room and have a good beefsteak.

CRAVEN (*shuddering*). Ugh! (*Plaintively*) No: I've lost my old manly taste for it. My very nature's been corrupted by living on pap. *(To Paramore.)* That's what comes of all this vivisection. You go experimenting on horses; and of course the result is that you try to get me into condition by feeding me on beans.

PARAMORE *(curtly, without changing his position).* Well, if they've done you good, so much the better for you.

CRAVEN *(querulously).* That's all very well; but it's very vexing. You don't half see how serious it is to make a man believe that he has only another year to live: you really don't, Paramore: I can't help saying it. I've made my will, which was altogether unnecessary; and I've been reconciled to a lot of people I'd quarrelled with—people I can't stand under ordinary circumstances. Then I've let the girls get round me at home to an extent I should never have done if I'd had my life before me. I've done a lot of serious thinking and reading and extra church going. And now it turns out simple waste of time. On my soul, it's too disgusting: I'd far rather die like a man when I said I would.

PARAMORE *(as before).* Perhaps you may. Your heart's shaky, if that's any satisfaction to you.

CRAVEN *(offended).* You must excuse me, Paramore, if I say that I no longer feel any confidence in your opinion as a medical man. *(Paramore's eye flashes: he straightens himself and listens.)* I paid you a pretty stiff fee for that consultation when you condemned me; and I can't say I think you gave me value for it.

PARAMORE *(turning and facing Craven with dignity).* That's unanswerable, Colonel Craven. I shall return the fee.

CRAVEN. Oh, it's not the money; but I think you ought to realize your position. *(Paramore turns stiffly away. Craven follows him impulsively, exclaiming remorsefully)* Well, perhaps it was a nasty thing of me to allude to it. *(He offers Paramore his hand.)*

PARAMORE *(conscientiously taking it).* Not at all. You are quite in the right, Colonel Craven. My diagnosis was wrong; and I must take the consequences.

CRAVEN *(holding his hand).* No, don't say that. It was natural enough: my liver is enough to set any man's diagnosis wrong. *(A long handshake, very trying to Paramore's nerves. Paramore then retires to the recess on Ibsen's left, and throws himself on the divan with a half suppressed sob, bending over the British Medical Journal with his head on his hands and his elbows on his knees.)*

CUTHBERTSON *(who has been rejoicing with Julia at the other side of the room).* Well, let's say no more about it. I congratulate you, Craven, and hope you may long be spared. *(Craven offers his hand.)* No, Dan: your daughter first. *(He takes Julia's hand gently and hands her across to Craven, into whose arms she flies with a gush of feeling.)*

JULIA. Dear old Daddy!

CRAVEN. Ah, is Julia glad that the old Dad is let off for a few years more?

JULIA *(almost crying).* Oh, so glad: so glad! *(Cuthbertson sobs audibly. The Colonel is affected. Sylvia, entering from the dining room, stops abruptly at the door on seeing the three. Paramore, in the recess, escapes her notice.)*

SYLVIA. Hallo!

CRAVEN. Tell her the news, Julia: it would sound ridiculous from me. *(He goes to the weeping Cuthbertson, and pats him consolingly on the shoulder.)*

JULIA. Silly: only think! Dad's not ill at all. It was only a mistake of Dr. Paramore's. Oh, dear! *(She catches Craven's left hand and stoops to kiss it, his right hand being still on Cuthbertson's shoulder.)*

SYLVIA *(contemptuously)*. I knew it. Of course it was nothing but eating too much. I always said Paramore was an ass. *(Sensation. Cuthbertson, Craven and Julia turn in consternation.)*

PARAMORE *(without malice)*. Never mind, Miss Craven. That is what is being said all over Europe now. Never mind.

SYLVIA *(a little abashed)*. I'm so sorry, Dr. Paramore. You must excuse a daughter's feelings.

CRAVEN *(huffed)*. It evidently doesn't make much difference to you, Sylvia.

SYLVIA. I'm not going to be sentimental over it, Dad, you may bet. *(Coming to Craven.)* Besides, I knew it was nonsense all along. *(Petting him.)* Poor dear old Dad! why should your days be numbered any more than any one else's? *(He pats her cheek, mollified. Julia impatiently turns away from them.)* Come to the smoking room, and let's see what you can do after teetotalling for a year.

CRAVEN *(playfully)*. Vulgar little girl! *(He pinches her ear.)* Shall we come, Jo! You'll be the better for a pick-me-up after all this emotion.

CUTHBERTSON. I'm not ashamed of it, Dan. It has done me good. *(He goes up to the table and shakes his fist at the bust over the mantelpiece.)* It would do you good too if you had eyes and ears to take it in.

CRAVEN *(astonished)*. Who?

SYLVIA. Why, good old Henrik, of course.

CRAVEN *(puzzled)*. Henrik?

CUTHBERTSON *(impatiently)*. Ibsen, man: Ibsen. *(He goes out by the staircase door followed by Sylvia, who kisses her hand to the bust as she passes. Craven stares blankly after her, and then up at the bust. Giving the problem up as insoluble, he shakes his head and follows them. Near the door he checks himself and comes back.)*

CRAVEN *(softly)*. By the way, Paramore?—

PARAMORE *(rousing himself with an effort)*. Yes?

CRAVEN. You weren't in earnest that time about my heart, were you?

PARAMORE. Oh, nothing, nothing. There's a slight murmur—mitral valves a little worn, perhaps; but they'll last your time if you're careful. Don't smoke too much.

CRAVEN. What! More privations! Now really, Paramore, really—

PARAMORE *(rising distractedly)*. Excuse me: I can't pursue the subject. I— I—

JULIA. Don't worry him now, Daddy.

CRAVEN. Well, well: I won't. *(He comes to Paramore, who is pacing restlessly up and down the middle of the room.)* Come, Paramore, I'm not selfish, believe me: I can feel for your disappointment. But you must face it like a man. And after all, now really, doesn't this shew that there's a lot of rot about modern science? Between ourselves, you know, it's horribly cruel: you must admit that it's a deuced nasty thing to go ripping up and crucifying camels and monkeys. It must blunt all the finer feelings sooner or later.

PARAMORE *(turning on him)*. How many camels and horses and men were ripped up in that Soudan campaign where you won your Victoria Cross, Colonel Craven?

CRAVEN *(firing up)*. That was fair fighting—a very different thing, Paramore.

PARAMORE. Yes, Martinis and machine guns against naked spearmen.

CRAVEN *(hotly)*. I took my chance with the rest, Dr. Paramore. I risked my own life: don't forget that.

PARAMORE *(with equal spirit)*. And I have risked mine, as all doctors do, oftener than any soldier.

CRAVEN. That's true. I didn't think of that. I beg your pardon, Paramore: I'll never say another word against your profession. But I hope you'll let me stick to the good old-fashioned shaking up treatment for my liver—a clinking run across country with the hounds.

PARAMORE *(with bitter irony)*. Isn't that rather cruel—a pack of dogs ripping up a fox?

JULIA *(coming coaxingly between them)*. Oh, please don't begin arguing again. Do go to the smoking room, Daddy: Mr. Cuthbertson will wonder what has become of you.

CRAVEN. Very well, very well: I'll go. But you're really not reasonable to-day, Paramore, to talk that way of fair sport—

JULIA. Sh—sh *(coaxing him toward the door)*.

CRAVEN. Well, well, I'm off. *(He goes good-humoredly, pushed out by Julia.)*

JULIA *(turning at the door with her utmost witchery of manner)*. Don't look so disappointed, Dr. Paramore. Cheer up. You've been most kind to us; and you've done papa a lot of good.

PARAMORE *(delighted, rushing over to her)*. How beautiful it is of you to say that to me, Miss Craven!

JULIA. I hate to see any one unhappy. I can't bear unhappiness. *(She runs out, casting a Parthian glance at him as she flies. Paramore stands enraptured, gazing after her through the glass door. Whilst he is thus absorbed Charteris comes in from the dining room and touches him on the arm.)*

PARAMORE *(starting)*. Eh! What's the matter?

CHARTERIS *(significantly)*. Charming woman, isn't she, Paramore? *(Looking admiringly at him.)* How have you managed to fascinate her?

PARAMORE. I! Do you really mean— *(He looks at him; then recovers himself and adds coldly.)* Excuse me: this is a subject I do not care to jest about. *(He walks away from Charteris down the side of the room, and sits down in an easy chair reading his Journal to intimate that he does not wish to pursue the conversation.)*

CHARTERIS *(ignoring the hint and coolly taking a chair beside him)*. Why don't you get married, Paramore? You know it's a scandalous thing for a man in your profession to be single.

PARAMORE *(shortly, still pretending to read)*. That's my own business, not yours.

CHARTERIS. Not at all: it's pre-eminently a social question. You're going to get married, aren't you?

PARAMORE. Not that I am aware of.

CHARTERIS *(alarmed)*. No! Don't say that. Why?

PARAMORE *(rising angrily and rapping one of the SILENCE placards)*. Allow me to call your attention to that. *(He crosses to the easy chair near the revolving bookstand, and flings himself into it with determined hostility.)*

CHARTERIS *(following him, too deeply concerned to mind the rebuff)*. Paramore: you alarm me more than I can say. You've been and muffed this business somehow. I know perfectly well what you've been up to; and I fully expected to find you a joyful accepted suitor.

PARAMORE *(angrily)*. Yes, you have been watching me because you admire Miss Craven yourself. Well, you may go in and win now. You will be pleased to hear that I am a ruined man.

CHARTERIS. You! Ruined! How? The turf?

PARAMORE *(contemptuously)*. The turf!! Certainly not.

CHARTERIS. Paramore: if the loan of all I possess will help you over this difficulty, you're welcome to it.

PARAMORE *(rising in surprise)*. Charteris! I— *(suspiciously.)* Are you joking?

CHARTERIS. Why on earth do you always suspect me of joking? I never was more serious in my life.

PARAMORE *(shamed by Charteris's generosity)*. Then I beg your pardon. I thought the news would please you.

CHARTERIS *(deprecating this injustice to his good feeling)*. My dear fellow—!

PARAMORE. I see I was wrong. I am really very sorry. *(They shake hands.)* And now you may as well learn the truth. I had rather you heard it from me than from the gossip of the club. My liver discovery has been—er—er—*(he cannot bring himself to say it)*.

CHARTERIS *(helping him out)*. Confirmed? *(Sadly.)* I see: the poor Colonel's doomed.

PARAMORE. No: on the contrary, it has been—er—called in question. The Colonel now believes himself to be in perfectly good health; and my friendly relations with the Cravens are entirely spoiled.

CHARTERIS. Who told him about it?

PARAMORE. I did, of course, the moment I read the news in this. *(He shews the Journal and puts it down on the bookstand.)*

CHARTERIS. Why, man, you've been a messenger of glad tidings! Didn't you congratulate him?

PARAMORE *(scandalised)*. Congratulate him! Congratulate a man on the worst blow pathological science has received for the last three hundred years!

CHARTERIS. No, no, no. Congratulate him on having his life saved. Congratulate Julia on having her father spared. Swear that your discovery and your reputation are as nothing to you compared with the pleasure of restoring happiness to the household in which the best hopes of your life are centred. Confound it, man, you'll never get married if you can't turn things to account with a woman in these little ways.

PARAMORE (*gravely*). Excuse me; but my self-respect is dearer to me even than Miss Craven. I cannot trifle with scientific questions for the sake of a personal advantage. (*He turns away coldly and goes toward the table.*)

CHARTERIS. Well, this beats me! The nonconformist conscience is bad enough; but the scientific conscience is the very devil. (*He follows Paramore and puts his arm familiarly round his shoulder, bringing him back again whilst he speaks.*) Now look here, Paramore: I've got no conscience in that sense at all: I loathe it as I loathe all the snares of idealism; but I have some common humanity and common sense. (*He replaces him in the easy chair and sits down opposite him.*) Come: what is a really scientific theory?—a true theory, isn't it?

PARAMORE. No doubt.

CHARTERIS. For instance, you have a theory about Craven's liver, eh?

PARAMORE. I still believe that to be a true theory, though it has been upset for the moment.

CHARTERIS. And you have a theory that it would be pleasant to be married to Julia?

PARAMORE. I suppose so—in a sense.

CHARTERIS. That theory also will be upset, probably, before you're a year older.

PARAMORE. Always cynical, Charteris.

CHARTERIS. Never mind that. Now it's a perfectly damnable thing for you to hope that your liver theory is true, because it amounts to hoping that Craven will die an agonizing death. (*This strikes Paramore as paradoxical; but it startles him.*) But it's amiable and human to hope that your theory about Julia is right, because it amounts to hoping that she may live happily ever after.

PARAMORE. I do hope that with all my soul—(*correcting himself*) I mean with all my function of hoping.

CHARTERIS. Then, since both theories are equally scientific, why not devote yourself, as a humane man, to proving the amiable theory rather than the damnable one?

PARAMORE. But how?

CHARTERIS. I'll tell you. You think I'm fond of Julia myself. So I am; but then I'm fond of everybody; so I don't count. Besides, if you try the scientific experiment of asking her whether she loves me, she'll tell you that she hates and despises me. So I'm out of the running. Nevertheless, like you, I hope that she may be happy with all my—what did you call your soul?

PARAMORE (*impatiently*). Oh, go on, go on: finish what you were going to say.

CHARTERIS (*suddenly affecting complete indifference, and rising carelessly*). I don't know that I have anything more to say. If I were you I should invite the Cravens to tea in honor of the Colonel's escape from a horrible doom. By the way, if you've done with that British Medical Journal, I should like to see how they've smashed your theory up.

PARAMORE (*wincing as he also rises*). Oh, certainly, if you wish it. I have no objection. *(He takes the Journal from the bookstand.)* I admit that the Italian experiments apparently upset my theory. But please remember that it is doubtful—extremely doubtful—whether anything can be proved by experiments on animals. *(He hands Charteris the Journal.)*

CHARTERIS *(taking it).* It doesn't matter: I don't intend to make any. *(He retires to the recess on Ibsen's right, picking up the step ladder as he passes and placing it so that he is able to use it for a leg rest as he settles himself to read on the divan with his back to the corner of the mantelpiece. Paramore goes to the left hand door, and is about to leave the library when he meets Grace entering.)*

GRACE. How do you do, Dr. Paramore. So glad to see you. *(They shake hands.)*

PARAMORE. Thanks. Quite well, I hope?

GRACE. Quite, thank you. You're looking overworked. We must take more care of you, Doctor.

PARAMORE. You are very kind.

GRACE. It is you who are too kind—to your patients. You sacrifice yourself. Have a little rest. Come and talk to me—tell me all about the latest scientific discoveries, and what I ought to read to keep myself up to date. But perhaps you're busy.

PARAMORE. No, not at all. Only too delighted. *(They go into the recess on Ibsen's left, and sit there chatting in whispers, very confidentially.)*

CHARTERIS. How they all love a doctor! They can say what they like to him! *(Julia returns. He takes his feet down from the ladder and sits up.)* Whew! *(Julia wanders down his side of the room, apparently looking for someone. Charteris steals after her.)*

CHARTERIS *(in a low voice).* Looking for me, Julia?

JULIA *(starting violently).* Oh! How you startled me!

CHARTERIS. Sh! I want to shew you something. Look! *(He points to the pair in the recess.)*

JULIA *(jealously).* That woman!

CHARTERIS. My young woman, carrying off your young man.

JULIA. What do you mean? Do you dare insinuate—

CHARTERIS. Sh—sh—sh! Don't disturb them. *(Paramore rises; takes down a book; and sits on a footstool at Grace's feet.)*

JULIA. Why are they whispering like that?

CHARTERIS. Because they don't want anyone to hear what they are saying to one another. *(Paramore shews Grace a picture in the book. They both laugh heartily over it.)*

JULIA. What is he shewing her?

CHARTERIS. Probably a diagram of the liver. *(Julia, with an exclamation of disgust makes for the recess. Charteris catches her sleeve.)* Stop: be careful, Julia. *(She frees herself by giving him a push which upsets him into the easy chair; then crosses to the recess and stands looking down at Grace and Paramore from the corner next the fireplace.)*

JULIA *(with suppressed fury).* You seem to have found a very interesting book, Dr. Paramore. *(They look up, astonished.)* May I ask what it is? *(She stoops swiftly; snatches the book from Paramore; and comes down to the table quickly to look at it whilst they rise in amazement.*) Good Words! (*She flings it on the table and sweeps back past Charteris, exclaiming contemptuously*) You fool! (*Paramore and Grace, meanwhile, come from the recess; Paramore bewildered, Grace very determined.*)

CHARTERIS (*aside to Julia as he gets out of the easy chair*). Idiot! She'll have you turned out of the club for this.

JULIA (*terrified*). She can't—can she?

PARAMORE. What is the matter, Miss Craven?

CHARTERIS (*hastily*). Nothing—my fault—a stupid, practical joke. I beg your pardon and Mrs. Tranfield's.

GRACE (*firmly*). It is not your fault in the least, Mr. Charteris. Dr. Paramore: will you oblige me by finding Sylvia Craven for me, if you can?

PARAMORE (*hesitating*). But—

GRACE. I want you to go now, if you please.

PARAMORE (*succumbing*). Certainly. (*He bows and goes out by the staircase door.*)

GRACE. You are going with him, Charteris.

JULIA. You will not leave me here to be insulted by this woman, Mr. Charteris. (*She takes his arm as if to go with him.*)

GRACE. When two ladies quarrel in this club, it is against the rules to settle it when there are gentlemen present—especially the gentleman they are quarrelling about. I presume you do not wish to break that rule, Miss Craven. (*Julia sullenly drops Charteris's arm. Grace turns to Charteris and adds*) Now! Trot off.

CHARTERIS. Certainly, certainly. (*He follows Paramore ignominiously.*)

GRACE (*to Julia, with quiet peremptoriness*). Now: what have you to say to me?

JULIA (*suddenly throwing herself tragically on her knees at Grace's feet*). Don't take him from me. Oh don't—don't be so cruel. Give him back to me. You don't know what you're doing—what our past has been—how I love him. You don't know—

GRACE. Get up; and don't be a fool. Suppose anyone comes in and sees you in that ridiculous attitude!

JULIA. I hardly know what I'm doing. I don't care what I'm doing: I'm too miserable. Oh, won't you listen to me?

GRACE. Do you suppose I am a man to be imposed on by this sort of rubbish?

JULIA (*getting up and looking darkly at her*). You intend to take him from me, then?

GRACE. Do you expect me to help you to keep him after the way you have behaved?

JULIA (*trying her theatrical method in a milder form—reasonable and impulsively goodnatured instead of tragic*). I know I was wrong to act as I did last night. I beg your pardon. I am sorry. I was mad.

GRACE. Not a bit mad. You calculated to an inch how far you could go. When he is present to stand between us and play out the scene with you, I count for nothing. When we are alone you fall back on your natural way of getting anything you want—crying for it like a baby until it is given to you.

JULIA (*with unconcealed hatred*). You learnt this from him.

GRACE. I learnt it from yourself, last night and now. How I hate to be a woman when I see, by you, what wretched childish creatures we are! Those two men would cut you dead and have you turned out of the club if you were a man and had behaved in such a way before them. But because you are only a woman, they are forbearing, sympathetic, gallant—Oh, if you had a scrap of self-respect, their indulgence would make you creep all over. I understand now why Charteris has no respect for women.

JULIA. How dare you say that?

GRACE. Dare! I love him. And I have refused his offer to marry me.

JULIA (incredulous but hopeful). You have refused!

GRACE. Yes: because I will not give myself to any man who has learnt how to treat women from you and your like. I can do without his love, but not without his respect; and it is your fault that I cannot have both. Take his love then; and much good may it do you! Run to him and beg him to have mercy on you and take you back.

JULIA. Oh, what a liar you are! He loved me before he ever saw you—before he ever dreamt of you, you pitiful thing. Do you think I need go down on my knees to men to make them come to me? That may be your experience, you creature with no figure: it is not mine. There are dozens of men who would give their souls for a look from me. I have only to lift my finger.

GRACE. Lift it then; and see whether he will come.

JULIA. How I should like to kill you! I don't know why I don't.

GRACE. Yes: you like to get out of your difficulties cheaply—at other people's expense. It is something to boast of, isn't it, that dozens of men would make love to you if you invited them?

JULIA (sullenly). I suppose it's better to be like you, with a cold heart and a serpent's tongue. Thank Heaven, I have a heart: that is why you can hurt me as I cannot hurt you. And you are a coward. You are giving him up to me without a struggle.

GRACE. Yes, it is for you to struggle. I wish you success. (She turns away contemptuously and is going to the dining-room door when Sylvia enters on the opposite side, followed by Cuthbertson and Craven, who come to Julia, whilst Sylvia crosses to Grace.)

SYLVIA. Here I am, sent by the faithful Paramore. He hinted that I'd better bring the elder members of the family too: here they are. What's the row?

GRACE (quietly). Nothing, dear. There's no row.

JULIA (hysterically, tottering and stretching out her arms to Craven). Daddy!

CRAVEN (taking her in his arms). My precious! What's the matter?

JULIA (through her tears). She's going to have me expelled from the club; and we shall all be disgraced. Can she do it, Daddy?

CRAVEN. Well, really, the rules of this club are so extraordinary that I don't know. (To Grace.) May I ask, Mrs. Tranfield, whether you have any complaint to make of my daughter's conduct?

GRACE. Yes, Colonel Craven. I am going to complain to the committee.

SYLVIA. I knew you'd overdo it some day, Julia. (Craven, at a loss, looks at Cuthbertson.)

CUTHBERTSON. Don't look at me, Dan. Within these walls a father's influence counts for nothing.

CRAVEN. May I ask the ground of complaint, Mrs. Tranfield?

GRACE. Simply that Miss Craven is essentially a womanly woman, and, as such, not eligible for membership.

JULIA. It's false. I'm not a womanly woman. I was guaranteed when I joined just as you were.

GRACE. By Mr. Charteris, I think, at your own request. I shall call him as a witness to your thoroughly womanly conduct just now in his presence and Dr. Paramore's.

CRAVEN. Cuthbertson: are they joking; or am I dreaming?

CUTHBERTSON (grimly). It's real, Dan: you're awake.

SYLVIA (taking Craven's left arm and hugging it affectionately). Dear old Rip Van Winkle!

CRAVEN. Well, Mrs. Tranfield, all I can say is that I hope you will succeed in establishing your complaint, and that Julia may soon see the last of this most outrageous institution. (Sylvia, still caressing his arm, laughs at him; Charteris returns.)

CHARTERIS (at the door). May I come in?

SYLVIA (releasing the Colonel). Yes: you're wanted here as a witness. (Charteris comes in.) It's a bad case of womanliness.

GRACE (half aside to him, significantly). You understand. (Julia, watching them jealously, leaves her father and gets close to Charteris. Grace adds aloud) I shall expect your support before the committee.

JULIA. If you have a scrap of manhood you will take my part.

CHARTERIS. But then I shall be expelled for being a manly man. Besides, I'm on the committee myself; I can't act as judge and witness, too. You must apply to Paramore: he saw it all.

GRACE. Where is Dr. Paramore?

CHARTERIS. Just gone home.

JULIA (with sudden resolution). What is Dr. Paramore's number in Savile Row?

CHARTERIS. Seventy-nine. (Julia goes out quickly by the staircase door, to their astonishment. Charteris follows her to the door, which swings back in his face, leaving him staring after her through, the glass. Sylvia runs to Grace.)

SYLVIA. Grace: go after her. Don't let her get beforehand with Paramore. She'll tell him the most heartbreaking stories about how she's been treated, and get him round completely.

CRAVEN (floundering). Sylvia! Is that the way to speak of your sister, miss? (Grace squeezes Sylvia's hand to console her, and sits down calmly. Sylvia posts herself behind Grace's chair, leaning over the back to watch the ensuing colloquy between the three men.) I assure you, Mrs. Tranfield, Dr. Paramore has just invited us all to take afternoon tea with him; and if my daughter has gone to his house, she is simply taking advantage of his invitation to extricate herself from a very embarrassing scene here. We're all going there. Come, Sylvia. (He turns to go, followed by Cuthbertson.)

CHARTERIS (in consternation). Stop! (He gets between Craven and Cuthbertson.) What hurry is there? Can't you give the man time?

CRAVEN. Time! What for?

CHARTERIS (*talking foolishly in his agitation*). Well, to get a little rest, you know—a busy professional man like that! He's not had a moment to himself all day.

CRAVEN. But Julia's with him.

CHARTERIS. Well, no matter: she's only one person. And she ought to have an opportunity of laying her case before him. As a member of the committee, I think that's only just. Be reasonable, Craven: give him half an hour.

CUTHBERTSON (*sternly*). What do you mean by this, Charteris?

CHARTERIS. Nothing, I assure you. Only common consideration for poor Paramore.

CUTHBERTSON. You've some motive. Craven: I strongly advise that we go at once. (*He grasps the door handle.*)

CHARTERIS (*coaxingly*). No, no. (*He puts his hand persuasively on Craven's arm, adding*) It's not good for your liver, Craven, to rush about immediately after lunch.

CUTHBERTSON. His liver's cured. Come on. Craven. (*He opens the door.*)

CHARTERIS (*catching Cuthbertson by the sleeve*). Cuthbertson, you're mad. Paramore's going to propose to Julia. We must give him time: he's not the man to come to the point in three minutes as you or I would. (*Turning to Craven*) Don't you see?—that will get me out of the difficulty we were speaking of this morning—you and I and Cuthbertson. You remember?

CRAVEN. Now, is this a thing to say plump out before everybody, Charteris? Confound it, have you no decency?

CUTHBERTSON (*severely*). None whatever.

CHARTERIS (*turning to Cuthbertson*). No—don't be unkind, Cuthbertson. Back me up. My future, her future, Mrs. Tranfield's future, Craven's future, everybody's future depends on our finding Julia Paramore's affianced bride when we go over to Savile Row. He's certain to propose if you'll only give him time. You know you're a kindly and sensible man as well as a deucedly clever one, Cuthbertson, in spite of all your nonsense. Say a word for me.

CRAVEN. I'm quite willing to leave the decision to Cuthbertson; and I have no doubt whatever as to what that decision will be. (*Cuthbertson carefully shuts the door, and comes back into the room with an air of weighty reflection.*)

CUTHBERTSON. I am now going to speak as a man of the world: that is, without moral responsibility.

CRAVEN. Quite so, Jo. Of course.

CUTHBERTSON. Therefore, though I have no sympathy whatever with Charteris's views, I think we can do no harm by waiting—say ten minutes or so. (*He sits down.*)

CHARTERIS (*delighted*). Ah, there's nobody like you after all, Cuthbertson, when there's a difficult situation to be judged.

CRAVEN (*deeply disappointed*). Oh, well, Jo, if that is your decision, I must keep my word and abide by it. Better sit down and make ourselves comfortable, I suppose. (*He sits also, under protest.*)

CHARTERIS *(fidgeting about)*. I can't sit down: I'm too restless. The fact is, Julia has made me so nervous that I can't answer for myself until I know her decision. Mrs. Tranfield will tell you what a time I've had lately. Julia's really a most determined woman, you know.

CRAVEN *(starting up)*. Well, upon my life! Upon my honor and conscience!! Now really!!! I shall go this instant. Come on, Sylvia. Cuthbertson: I hope you'll mark your sense of this sort of thing by coming on to Paramore's with us at once. *(He marches to the door.)*

CHARTERIS *(desperately)*. Craven: you're trifling with your daughter's happiness. I only ask five minutes more.

CRAVEN. Not five seconds, sir. Fie for shame, Charteris! *(He goes out.)*

CUTHBERTSON *(to Charteris, as he passes him on his way to the door)*. Bungler! *(He follows Craven.)*

SYLVIA. Serve you right, you duffer! *(She follows Cuthbertson.)*

CHARTERIS. Oh, these headstrong old men! *(To Grace)* Nothing to be done now but go with them and delay the Colonel as much as possible. So I'm afraid I must leave you.

GRACE *(rising)*. Not at all. Paramore invited me, too, when we were talking over there.

CHARTERIS *(aghast)*. You don't mean to say you're coming!

GRACE. Most certainly. Do you suppose I will let that woman think I am afraid to meet her? *(Charteris sinks on a chair with a prolonged groan.)* Come: don't be silly: you'll not overtake the Colonel if you delay any longer.

CHARTERIS. Why was I ever born, child of misfortune that I am! *(He rises despairingly.)* Well, if you must come, you must. *(He offers his arm, which she takes.)* By the way, what happened after I left you?

GRACE. I gave her a lecture on her behavior which she will remember to the last day of her life.

CHARTERIS *(approvingly)*. That was right, darling. *(He slips his arm round her waist.)* Just one kiss—to soothe me.

GRACE *(complacently offering her cheek)*. Foolish boy! *(He kisses her.)* Now come along. *(They go out together.)*

END OF ACT III.

ACT IV

SITTING-room in Paramore's apartments in Savile Row. The darkly respectable furniture is, so to speak, en suite with Paramore's frock coat and cuffs. Viewing the room from the front windows, the door is seen in the opposite wall near the left hand corner. Another door, a light, noiseless partition one covered with a green baize, is in the right hand wall toward the back, leading to Paramore's consulting room. The fireplace is on the left. At the nearest corner of it a couch is placed at right angles to the wall, settlewise. On the right the wall is occupied by a bookcase, further forward than the green baize door. Beyond the door is a cabinet of anatomical preparations, with a framed photograph of Rembrandt's School of Anatomy hanging on the wall above it. In front, a little to the right, a tea-table.

Paramore is seated in a round-backed chair, on castors, pouring out tea. Julia sits opposite him, with her back to the fire. He is in high spirits: she very downcast.

PARAMORE *(handing her the cup he has just filled)*. There! Making tea is one of the few things I consider myself able to do thoroughly well. Cake?

JULIA. No, thank you. I don't like sweet things. *(She sets down the cup untasted.)*

PARAMORE. Anything wrong with the tea?

JULIA. No, it's very nice.

PARAMORE. I'm afraid I'm a very bad entertainer. The fact is, I'm too professional. I only shine in consultation. I almost wish you had something the matter with you; so that you might call out my knowledge and sympathy. As it is, I can only admire you, and feel how pleasant it is to have you here.

JULIA *(bitterly)*. And pet me, and say pretty things to me! I wonder you don't offer me a saucer of milk at once?

PARAMORE *(astonished)*. Why?

JULIA. Because you seem to regard me very much as if I were a Persian cat.

PARAMORE *(in strong remonstrance)*. Miss Cra—

JULIA *(cutting him short)*. Oh, you needn't protest. I'm used to it: It's the only sort of attachment I seem always to inspire. *(Ironically)* You can't think how flattering it is!

PARAMORE. My dear Miss Craven, what a cynical thing to say! You! who are loved at first sight by the people in the street as you pass. Why, in the club I can tell by the faces of the men whether you have been lately in the room or not.

JULIA *(shrinking fiercely)*. Oh, I hate that look in their faces. Do you know that I have never had one human being care for me since I was born?

PARAMORE. That's not true, Miss Craven. Even if it were true of your father, and of Charteris, who loves you madly in spite of your dislike for him, it is not true of me.

JULIA *(startled)*. Who told you that about Charteris?

PARAMORE. Why, he himself.

JULIA (*with deep, poignant conviction*). He cares for only one person in the world; and that is himself. There is not in his whole nature one unselfish spot. He would not spend one hour of his real life with— (*a sob chokes her: she rises passionately, crying*) You are all alike, every one of you. Even my father only makes a pet of me. (*She goes away to the fireplace and stands with her back to him.*)

PARAMORE (*following her humbly*). I don't deserve this from you: indeed I do not.

JULIA (*rating him*). Then why do you talk about me with Charteris, behind my back?

PARAMORE. We said nothing disparaging of you. Nobody shall ever do that in my presence. We spoke of the subject nearest our hearts.

JULIA. His heart! Oh, God, his heart! (*She sits down on the couch and hides her face.*)

PARAMORE (*sadly*). I am afraid you love him, for all that, Miss Craven.

JULIA (*raising her head instantly*). If he says that, he lies. If ever you hear it said that I cared for him, contradict it: it is false.

PARAMORE (*quickly advancing to her*). Miss Craven: is the way clear for me then?

JULIA (*pettishly—losing interest in the conversation and looking crossly into the fire*). What do you mean?

PARAMORE (*impetuously*). You must see what I mean. Contradict the rumour of your attachment to Charteris, not by words—it has gone too far for that—but by becoming my wife. (*Earnestly.*) Believe me: it is not merely your beauty that attracts me: (*Julia, interested, looks up at him quickly*) I know other beautiful women. It is your heart, your sincerity, your sterling reality, (*Julia rises and gazes at him, breathless with a new hope*) your great gifts of character that are only half developed because you have never been understood by those about you.

JULIA (*looking intently at him, and yet beginning to be derisively sceptical in spite of herself*). Have you really seen all that in me?

PARAMORE. I have felt it. I have been alone in the world; and I need you, Julia. That is how I have divined that you, also, are alone in the world.

JULIA (*with theatrical pathos*). You are right there. I am indeed alone in the world.

PARAMORE (*timidly approaching her*). With you I should not be alone. And you?—with me?

JULIA. You! (*She gets quickly out of his reach, taking refuge at the tea-table.*) No, no. I can't bring myself— (*She breaks off, perplexed, and looks uneasily about her.*) Oh, I don't know what to do. You will expect too much from me. (*She sits down.*)

PARAMORE. I have more faith in you than you have in yourself. Your nature is richer than you think.

JULIA (*doubtfully*). Do you really believe that I am not the shallow, jealous, devilish tempered creature they all pretend I am?

PARAMORE. I am ready to place my happiness in your hands. Does that prove what I think of you?

JULIA. Yes: I believe you really care for me. (*He approaches her eagerly: she has a violent revulsion, and rises with her hand raised as if to beat him off, crying)* No, no, no, no. I cannot. It's impossible. *(She goes towards the door.)*

PARAMORE *(looking wistfully after her)*. Is it Charteris?

JULIA *(stopping and turning)*. Ah, you think that! *(She comes back.)* Listen to me. If I say yes, will you promise not to touch me—to give me time to accustom myself to the idea of our new relations?

PARAMORE. I promise most faithfully. I would not press you for the world.

JULIA. Then—then—yes: I promise. *(He is about to utter his rapture; she will not have it.)* Now, not another word of it. Let us forget it. *(She resumes her seat at the table.)* Give me some more tea. *(He hastens to his former seat. As he passes, she puts her left hand on his arm and says)* Be good to me, Percy, I need it sorely.

PARAMORE *(transported)*. You have called me Percy! Hurrah! *(Charteris and Craven come in. Paramore hastens to meet them, beaming.)* Delighted to see you here with me, Colonel Craven. And you, too, Charteris. Sit down. *(The Colonel sits down on the end of the couch.)* Where are the others?

CHARTERIS. Sylvia has dragged Cuthbertson off into the Burlington Arcade to buy some caramels. He likes to encourage her in eating caramels: he thinks it's a womanly taste. Besides, he likes them himself. They'll be here presently. *(He strolls across to the cabinet and pretends to study the Rembrandt photograph, so as to be as far out of Julia's reach as possible.)*

CRAVEN. Yes; and Charteris has been trying to persuade me that there's a short cut between Cork Street and Savile Row somewhere in Conduit Street. Now did you ever hear such nonsense? Then he said my coat was getting shabby, and wanted me to go into Poole's and order a new one. Paramore: is my coat shabby?

PARAMORE. Not that I can see.

CRAVEN. I should think not. Then he wanted to draw me into a dispute about the Egyptian war. We should have been here quarter of an hour ago only for his nonsense.

CHARTERIS *(still contemplating Rembrandt)*. I did my best to keep him from disturbing you, Paramore.

PARAMORE *(gratefully)*. You have come in the nick of time. Colonel Craven: I have something very particular to say to you.

CRAVEN *(springing up in alarm)*. In private, Paramore: now really it must be in private.

PARAMORE *(surprised)*. Of course. I was about to suggest my consulting room: there's nobody there. Miss Craven: will you excuse me: Charteris will entertain you until I return. *(He leads the way to the green baize door.)*

CHARTERIS *(aghast)*. Oh, I say, hadn't you better wait until the others come?

PARAMORE *(exultant)*. No need for further delay now, my best friend. *(He wrings Charteris's hand.)* Will you come, Colonel?

CRAVEN. At your service, Paramore: at your service. *(Craven and Paramore go into the consulting room. Julia turns her head and stares insolently at Charteris. His nerves play him false: he is completely out of countenance in a moment. She rises suddenly. He starts, and comes hastily forward between the table and the bookcase. She crosses to that side behind the table; and he immediately crosses to the opposite side in front of it, dodging her.)*

CHARTERIS *(nervously)*. Don't, Julia. Now don't abuse your advantage. You've got me here at your mercy. Be good for once; and don't make a scene.

JULIA *(contemptuously)*. Do you suppose I am going to touch you?

CHARTERIS. No. Of course not. *(She comes forward on her side of the table. He retreats on his side of it. She looks at him with utter scorn; sweeps across to the couch; and sits down imperially. With a great sigh of relief he drops into Paramore's chair.)*

JULIA. Come here. I have something to say to you.

CHARTERIS. Yes? *(He rolls the chair a few inches towards her.)*

JULIA. Come here, I say. I am not going to shout across the room at you. Are you afraid of me?

CHARTERIS. Horribly. *(He moves the chair slowly, with great misgiving, to the end of the couch.)*

JULIA *(with studied insolence)*. Has that woman told you that she has given you up to me without an attempt to defend her conquest?

CHARTERIS *(whispering persuasively)*. Shew that you are capable of the same sacrifice. Give me up, too.

JULIA. Sacrifice! And so you think I'm dying to marry you, do you?

CHARTERIS. I am afraid your intentions have been honourable, Julia.

JULIA. You cad!

CHARTERIS *(with a sigh)*. I confess I am something either more or less than a gentleman, Julia. You once gave me the benefit of the doubt.

JULIA. Indeed! *I* never told you so. If you cannot behave like a gentleman, you had better go back to the society of the woman who has given you up—if such a cold-blooded, cowardly creature can be called a woman. *(She rises majestically; he makes his chair fly back to the table.)* I know you now, Leonard Charteris, through and through, in all your falseness, your petty spite, your cruelty and your vanity. The place you coveted has been won by a man more worthy of it.

CHARTERIS *(springing up, and coming close to her, gasping with eagerness)*. What do you mean? Out with it. Have you accep—

JULIA. I am engaged to Dr. Paramore.

CHARTERIS *(enraptured)*. My own Julia! *(He attempts to embrace her.)*

JULIA *(recoiling—he catching her hands and holding them)*. How dare you! Are you mad? Do you wish me to call Dr. Paramore?

CHARTERIS. Call everybody, my darling—everybody in London. Now I shall no longer have to be brutal—to defend myself—to go in fear of you. How I have looked forward to this day! You know now that I don't want you to marry me or to love me: Paramore can have all that. I only want to look on and rejoice disinterestedly in the happiness of *(kissing her hand)* my dear Julia *(kissing the other)*, my beautiful Julia. *(She tears her hands away and raises them as if to strike him, as she did the night before at Cuthbertson's.)* No use to threaten me now: I am not afraid of those hands—the loveliest hands in the world.

JULIA. How have you the face to turn round like this after insulting and torturing me!

CHARTERIS. Never mind, dearest: you never did understand me; and you never will. Our vivisecting friend has made a successful experiment at last.

JULIA (earnestly). It is you who are the vivisector—a far crueller, more wanton vivisector than he.

CHARTERIS. Yes; but then I learn so much more from my experiments than he does! And the victims learn as much as I do. That's where my moral superiority comes in.

JULIA (sitting down again on the couch with rueful humour). Well, you shall not experiment on me any more. Go to your Grace if you want a victim. She'll be a tough one.

CHARTERIS (reproachfully sitting down beside her). And you drove me to propose to her to escape from you! Suppose she had accepted me, where should I be now?

JULIA. Where I am, I suppose, now that I have accepted Paramore.

CHARTERIS. But I should have made Grace unhappy. (Julia sneers). However, now I come to think of it, you'll make Paramore unhappy. And yet if you refused him he would be in despair. Poor devil!

JULIA (her temper flashing up for a moment again). He is a better man than you.

CHARTERIS (humbly). I grant you that, my dear.

JULIA (impetuously). Don't call me your dear. And what do you mean by saying that I shall make him unhappy? Am I not good enough for him?

CHARTERIS (dubiously). Well, that depends on what you mean by good enough.

JULIA (earnestly). You might have made me good if you had chosen to. You had a great power over me. I was like a child in your hands; and you knew it.

CHARTERIS (with comic acquiescence). Yes, my dear. That means that whenever you got jealous and flew into a violent rage, I could always depend on it's ending happily if I only waited long enough, and petted you very hard all the time. When you had had your fling, and called the object of your jealousy every name you could lay your tongue to, and abused me to your heart's content for a couple of hours, then the reaction would come; and you would at last subside into a soothing rapture of affection which gave you a sensation of being angelically good and forgiving. Oh, I know that sort of goodness! You may have thought on these occasions that I was bringing out your latent amiability; but I thought you were bringing out mine, and using up rather more than your fair share of it.

JULIA. According to you, then, I have no good in me! I am an utterly vile, worthless woman. Is that it?

CHARTERIS. Yes, if you are to be judged as you judge others. From the conventional point of view, there's nothing to be said for you, Julia—nothing. That's why I have to find some other point of view to save my self-respect when I remember how I have loved you. Oh, what I have learnt from you!—from you, who could learn nothing from me! I made a fool of you; and you brought me wisdom: I broke your heart; and you brought me joy: I made you curse your womanhood; and you revealed my manhood to me. Blessings forever and ever on my Julia's name! *(With genuine emotion, he takes her hand to kiss it again.)*

JULIA *(snatching her hand away in disgust)*. Oh, stop talking that nasty sneering stuff.

CHARTERIS *(laughingly appealing to the heavens)*. She calls it nasty sneering stuff! Well, well: I'll never talk like that to you again, dearest. It only means that you are a beautiful woman, and that we all love you.

JULIA. Don't say that: I hate it. It sounds as if I were a mere animal.

CHARTERIS. Hm! A fine animal is a very wonderful thing. Don't let us disparage animals, Julia.

JULIA. That is what you really think me.

CHARTERIS. Come, Julia: you don't expect me to admire you for your moral qualities, do you? *(She turns and looks hard at him. He starts up apprehensively and backs away from her. She rises and follows him up slowly and intently.)*

JULIA *(deliberately)*. I have seen you very much infatuated with this depraved creature who has no moral qualities.

CHARTERIS *(retreating)*. Keep off, Julia. Remember your new obligations to Paramore.

JULIA *(overtaking him in the middle of the room)*. Never mind Paramore: that is my business. *(She grasps the lappels of his coat in her hands, and looks fixedly at him.)* Oh, if the people you talk so cleverly to could only know you as I know you! Sometimes I wonder at myself for ever caring for you.

CHARTERIS *(beaming at her)*. Only sometimes?

JULIA. You fraud! You humbug! You miserable little plaster saint! *(He looks delighted.)* Oh! *(In a paroxysm half of rage, half of tenderness, she shakes him, growling over him like a tigress over her cub. Paramore and Craven at this moment return from the consulting room, and are thunderstruck at the spectacle.)*

CRAVEN *(shouting, utterly scandalized)*. Julia!! *(Julia releases Charteris, but stands her ground disdainfully as they come forward, Craven on her left, Paramore on her right.)*

PARAMORE. What's the matter?

CHARTERIS. Nothing, nothing. You'll soon get used to this, Paramore.

CRAVEN. Now really, Julia, this is a very extraordinary way to behave. It's not fair to Paramore.

JULIA *(coldly)*. If Dr. Paramore objects he can break off our engagement. *(To Paramore)* Pray don't hesitate.

PARAMORE *(looking doubtfully and anxiously at her)*. Do you wish me to break it off?

CHARTERIS *(alarmed)*. Nonsense! don't act so hastily. It was my fault. I annoyed Miss Craven—insulted her. Hang it all, don't go and spoil everything like this.

CRAVEN. This is most infernally perplexing. I can't believe that you insulted Julia, Charteris. I've no doubt you annoyed her—you'd annoy anybody; upon my soul you would—but insult!—now what do you mean by that?

PARAMORE *(very earnestly)*. Miss Craven; delicacy and sincerity I ask you to be frank with me. What are the relations between you and Charteris?

JULIA. Ask him. (*She goes to the fireplace, her back on them.*)

CHARTERIS. Certainly: I'll confess. I'm in love with Miss Craven—always have been; and I've persecuted her with my addresses ever since I knew her. It's been no use: she utterly despises me. A moment ago the spectacle of a rival's happiness stung me to make a nasty, sneering speech; and she—well, she just shook me a little, as you saw.

PARAMORE (*chivalrously*).s I shall never forget that you helped me to win her, Charteris. (*Julia quickly, a spasm of fury in her face.*)

CHARTERIS. Sh! For Heaven's sake don't mention it.

CRAVEN. This is a very different story to the one you told Cuthbertson and myself this morning. You'll excuse my saying that it sounds much more like the the truth. Come: you were humbugging us, weren't you?

CHARTERIS. Ask Julia. (*Paramore and Craven turn to Julia. Charteris remains doggedly looking straight before him.*)

JULIA. It's quite true. He has been in love with me; he has persecuted me; and I utterly despise him.

GRAVEN. Don't rub it in, Julia: it's not kind. No man is quite himself when he's crossed in love. (*To Charteris.*) Now listen to me, Charteris. When I was a young fellow, Cuthbertson and I fell in love with the same woman. She preferred Cuthbertson. I was taken aback: I won't deny it. But I knew my duty; and I did it. I gave her up and wished Cuthbertson joy. He told me this morning, when we met after many years, that he has respected and liked me ever since for it. And I believe him and feel the better for it. (*Impressively.*) Now, Charteris, Paramore and you stand to-day where Cuthbertson and I stood on a certain July evening thirty-five years ago. How are you going to take it?

JULIA (*indignantly*). How is he going to take it, indeed! Really, papa, this is too much. If Mrs. Cuthbertson wouldn't have you, it may have been very noble of you to make a virtue of giving her up, just as you made a virtue of being a teetotaller when Percy cut off your wine. But he shan't be virtuous over me. I have refused him; and if he doesn't like it he can—he can—

CHARTERIS. I can lump it. Precisely. Craven: you can depend on me. I'll lump it. (*He moves off nonchalantly, and leans against the bookcase with his hands in his pockets.*)

CRAVEN (*hurt*). Julia: you don't treat me respectfully. I don't wish to complain; but that was not a becoming speech.

JULIA (*bursting into tears and throwing herself into the large chair*). Is there anyone in the world who has any feeling for me—who does not think me utterly vile? (*Craven and Paramore hurry to her in the greatest consternation.*)

CRAVEN (*remorsefully*). My pet: I didn't for a moment mean—

JULIA. Must I stand to be bargained for by two men—passed from one to the other like a slave in the market, and not say a word in my own defence?

CRAVEN. But, my love—

JULIA. Oh, go away, all of you. Leave me. I—oh— (*She gives way to a passion of tears.*)

PARAMORE (*reproachfully to Craven*). You've wounded her cruelly, Colonel Craven—cruelly.

CRAVEN. But I didn't mean to: I said nothing. Charteris: was I harsh?

CHARTERIS. You forget the revolt of the daughters, Craven. And you certainly wouldn't have gone on like that to any grown up woman who was not your daughter.

CRAVEN. Do you mean to say that I am expected to treat my daughter the same as I would any other girl?

PARAMORE. I should say certainly, Colonel Craven.

CRAVEN. Well, dash me if I will. There!

PARAMORE. If you take that tone, I have nothing more to say. (*He crosses the room with offended dignity and posts himself with his back to the bookcase beside Charteris.*)

JULIA (*with a sob*). Daddy.

CRAVEN (*turning solicitously to her*). Yes, my love.

JULIA (*looking up at him tearfully and kissing his hand*). Don't mind them. You didn't mean it, Daddy, did you?

CRAVEN. No, no, my precious. Come: don't cry.

PARAMORE (*to Charteris, looking at Julia with delight*). How beautiful she is!

CHARTERIS (*throwing up his hands*). Oh, Lord help you, Paramore! (*He leaves the bookcase and sits at the end of the couch farthest from the fire. Meanwhile Sylvia arrives.*)

SYLVIA (*contemplating Julia*). Crying again! Well, you are a womanly one!

CRAVEN. Don't worry your sister, Sylvia. You know she can't bear it.

SYLVIA. I speak for her good, Dad. All the world can't be expected to know that she's the family baby.

JULIA. You will get your ears boxed presently, Silly.

CRAVEN. Now, now, now, my dear children, really now! Come, Julia: put up your handkerchief before Mrs. Tranfield sees you. She's coming along with Jo.

JULIA (*rising*). That woman again!

SYLVIA. Another row! Go it, Julia!

CRAVEN. Hold your tongue, Sylvia. (*He turns commandingly to Julia.*) Now look here, Julia.

CHARTERIS. Hallo! A revolt of the fathers!

CRAVEN. Silence, Charteris. (*To Julia, unanswerably.*) The test of a man or woman's breeding is how they behave in a quarrel. Anybody can behave well when things are going smoothly. Now you said to-day, at that iniquitous club, that you were not a womanly woman. Very well: I don't mind. But if you are not going to behave like a lady when Mrs. Tranfield comes into this room, you've got to behave like a gentleman; or fond as I am of you, I'll cut you dead exactly as I would if you were my son.

PARAMORE (*remonstrating*). Colonel Craven—

CRAVEN (*cutting him short*). Don't be a fool, Paramore.

JULIA (*tearfully excusing herself*). I'm sure, Daddy—

CRAVEN. Stop snivelling. I'm not speaking as your Daddy now: I'm speaking as your commanding officer.

SYLVIA. Good old Victoria Cross! (*Craven turns sharply on her; and she darts away behind Charteris, and presently seats herself on the couch, so that she and Charteris are shoulder to shoulder, facing opposite ways. Cuthbertson arrives with Grace, who remains near the door whilst her father joins the others.*)

CRAVEN. Ah, Jo, here you are. Now, Paramore, tell 'em the news.

PARAMORE. Mrs. Tranfield—Cuthbertson—allow me to introduce you to my future wife.

CUTHBERTSON (*coming forward to shake hands with Paramore*). My heartiest congratulations! (*Paramore goes to shake hands with Grace.*) Miss Craven: you will accept Grace's congratulations as well as mine, I hope.

CRAVEN. She will, Jo. (*In a tone of command.*) Now, Julia. (*Julia slowly rises.*)

CUTHBERTSON. Now, Grace. (*He conducts her to Julia's right; then posts himself on the hearthrug, with his back to the fire, watching them. The Colonel keeps guard on the other side.*)

GRACE (*speaking in a low voice to Julia alone*). So you have shewn him that you can do without him! Now I take back everything I said. Will you shake hands with me? (*Julia gives her hand painfully, with her face averted.*) They think this a happy ending, Julia—these men—our lords and masters! (*The two stand silent, hand in hand.*)

SYLVIA (*leaning back across the couch, aside to Charteris*). Has she really chucked you? (*He nods assent. She looks at him dubiously, and adds*) I expect you chucked her.

CUTHBERTSON. And now, Paramore, mind you don't stand any chaff from Charteris about this. He's in the same predicament himself. He's engaged to Grace.

JULIA (*dropping Grace's hand, and speaking with breathless anguish, but not violently*). Again!

CHARTERIS (*rising hastily*). Don't be alarmed. It's all off.

SYLVIA (*rising indignantly*). What! You've chucked Grace too! What a shame! (*She goes to the other side of the room, fuming.*)

CHARTERIS (*following her and putting his hand soothingly on her shoulder*). She won't have me, old chap—that is (*turning to the others*) unless Mrs. Tranfield has changed her mind again.

GRACE. No: we shall remain very good friends, I hope; but nothing would induce me to marry you. (*She goes to chair above the fireplace and sits down with perfect composure.*)

JULIA. Ah! (*She sits down with a great sigh of relief.*)

SYLVIA (*consoling Charteris*). Poor old Leonard!

CHARTERIS. Yes: this is the doom of the philanderer. I shall have to go on philandering now all my life. No domesticity, no fireside, no little ones, nothing at all in Cuthbertson's line! Nobody will marry me—unless you, Sylvia—eh?

SYLVIA. Not if I know it, Charteris.

CHARTERIS (*to them all*). You see!

CRAVEN (*coming between Charteris and Sylvia*). Now you really shouldn't make a jest of these things: upon my life and soul you shouldn't, Charteris.

CUTHBERTSON (*on the hearthrug*). The only use he can find for sacred things is to make a jest of them. That's the New Order. Thank Heaven, we belong to the Old Order, Dan!

CHARTERIS. Cuthbertson: don't be symbolic.

CUTHBERTSON (*outraged*). Symbolic! That is an accusation of Ibsenism. What do you mean?

CHARTERIS. Symbolic of the Old Order. Don't persuade yourself that you represent the Old Order. There never was any Old Order.

CRAVEN. There I flatly contradict you and stand up for Jo. I'd no more have behaved as you do when I was a young man than I'd have cheated at cards. *I* belong to the Old Order.

CHARTERIS. You're getting old, Craven; and you want to make a merit of it, as usual.

CRAVEN. Come, now, Charteris: you're not offended, I hope. (*With a conciliatory outburst.*) Well, perhaps I shouldn't have said that about cheating at cards. I withdraw it (*offering his hand*).

CHARTERIS (*taking Craven's hand*). No offence, my dear Craven: none in the world. I didn't mean to shew any temper. But (*aside, after looking round to see whether the others are listening*) only just consider!—the spectacle of a rival's happiness!

CRAVEN (*aloud, decisively*). Charteris: now you've got to behave like a man. Your duty's plain before you. (*To Cuthbertson.*) Am I right, Jo?

CUTHBERTSON (*firmly*). You are, Dan.

CRAVEN (*to Charteris*). Go straight up and congratulate Julia. And do it like a gentleman, smiling.

CHARTERIS. Colonel: I will. Not a muscle shall betray the conflict within.

CRAVEN. Julia: Charteris has not congratulated you yet. He's coming to do it. (*Julia rises and fixes a dangerous look on Charteris.*)

SYLVIA (*whispering quickly behind Charteris as he is about to advance*). Take care. She's going to hit you. I know her. (*Charteris stops and looks cautiously at Julia, measuring the situation. They regard one another steadfastly for a moment. Grace softly rises and gets close to Julia.*)

CHARTERIS (*whispering over his shoulder to Sylvia*). I'll chance it. (*He walks confidently up to Julia.*) Julia? (*He proffers his hand.*)

JULIA (*exhausted, allowing herself to take it*). You are right. I am a worthless woman.

CHARTERIS (*triumphant, and gaily remonstrating*). Oh, why?

JULIA. Because I am not brave enough to kill you.

GRACE (*taking her in her arms as she sinks, almost fainting, away from him*). Oh, no. Never make a hero of a philanderer. (*Charteris, amused and untouched, shakes his head laughingly. The rest look at Julia with concern, and even a little awe, feeling for the first time the presence of a keen sorrow.*).